The Answer Is Simple . . .

Other Hay House Titles by Sonia Choquette

Books and Card Decks

The Answer Is Simple Oracle Cards
Ask Your Guides
Ask Your Guides Oracle Cards
Diary of a Psychic
The Intuitive Spark
Soul Lessons and Soul Purpose
Soul Lessons and Soul Purpose Oracle Cards
The Time Has Come . . . to Accept Your Intuitive Gifts
Trust Your Vibes
Trust Your Vibes at Work, and Let Them Work for You
Trust Your Vibes Oracle Cards
Vitamins for the Soul

CD Programs

Attunement to Higher Vibrational Living (4-CD set),
with Mark Stanton Welch

Meditations for Receiving Divine Guidance, Support, and Healing
(2-CD set)

How to Trust Your Vibes at Work and Let Them Work for You
(4-CD set)

Trust Your Vibes (6-CD set)

Please visit Hay House USA: **www.hayhouse.com**®
Hay House Australia: **www.hayhouse.com.au**
Hay House UK: **www.hayhouse.co.uk**
Hay House South Africa: **www.hayhouse.co.za**
Hay House India: **www.hayhouse.co.in**

The Answer Is Simple . . .

Love Yourself, Live Your Spirit!

SONIA CHOQUETTE

HAY HOUSE, INC.

Carlsbad, California • New York City
London • Sydney • Johannesburg
Vancouver • Hong Kong • New Delhi

Published and distributed in the United States by: Hay House, Inc.: www.
hayhouse.com • *Published and distributed in Australia by:* Hay House
Australia Pty. Ltd.: www.hayhouse.com.au • *Published and distributed in the
United Kingdom by:* Hay House UK, Ltd.: www.hayhouse.co.uk • *Published and
distributed in the Republic of South Africa by:* Hay House SA (Pty), Ltd.: www.
hayhouse.co.za • *Distributed in Canada by:* Raincoast: www.raincoast.com •
Published in India by: Hay House Publishers India: www.hayhouse.co.in

Editorial supervision: Jill Kramer • *Design:* Tricia Breidenthal

Library of Congress Cataloging-in-Publication Data

Choquette, Sonia.
  The answer is simple-- : love yourself, live your spirit! / Sonia Choquette. -- 1st
ed.
      p. cm.
  ISBN 978-1-4019-1736-4 (hardcover) -- ISBN 978-1-4019-1737-1 (pbk.) 1.
Parapsychology. 2. Spiritual life--Miscellanea. I. Title.
  BF1031.C515 2008
  131--dc22
                                        2007051761

Hardcover ISBN: 978-1-4019-1736-4
Tradepaper ISBN: 978-1-4019-1737-1

11 10 09 08   4 3 2 1
1st edition, September 2008

Printed in the United States of America

*I would like to dedicate
this book to my family—
Patrick, Sonia, and Sabrina,
who are quite simply my joy.*

Contents

Introduction

Ever since I was a child, I've worked intimately with others, guiding them through life's challenges and helping them find the most direct and satisfying path to fulfillment.

I've spoken with people around the world—in India, South Africa, Europe, Canada, South America, as well as the United States. I've talked with people with advanced academic and professional degrees, with those of the working class, and even with individuals who had no idea where their next meal was coming from.

I've spoken with young people, old people, single people, married people, divorced people, and widowed people. I've talked with folks who have lived charmed, graceful lives, as well as those who have suffered abominable tragedy. And in all of this, I've learned a thing or two myself:

1. The first thing I've learned is that life is school. We're here to discover how to overcome circumstances and create, with what we're given, the lives we really want.

2. I've also learned that if we work from ego, intellect, or emotion exclusively, we'll never successfully achieve our dreams.

Having observed thousands and thousands of people from virtually every walk of life, with every advantage or disadvantage, I can confidently say that the only ones who genuinely succeed, who find peace and joy in their hearts and take great pleasure in their life experiences, have a different way of going about things. Rather than relying solely on their egos—their defended, insecure personalities—and intellectual minds, suffering the assaults life renders them, they turn to a higher aspect of their nature, the Spirit within, and let this direct their lives.

Those who remember that we're Divine Spirit, and love and live in harmony with *their* Spirit, are the most successful individuals. People who love themselves and live their Spirit aren't necessarily subjected to any fewer challenges in life than those who rely solely on their egos and intellect to guide them. *Life is life.* For all of us, just when we're comfortable, an entirely new set of challenges or circumstances arises to which we must adapt—and often quickly.

No, loving and living the Spirit within doesn't prevent you from facing life's storms. It does, however, greatly assist you in navigating the treacherous waters as painlessly and creatively as possible. And it allows you to enjoy the journey while doing so.

The only problem is, so many of us are disconnected from our Spirit that we don't even know we have one to love, let alone live. If we're not aware of this part of us, we can't nurture it and trust it as the most essential component of our authentic self—our guiding light—so we remain stuck in a vicious cycle of fear and pain and miss out on the joy and creative wonder of living a Divine existence. This isn't what our Creator intended for us. The One Who made us meant for us to live creative lives filled with joy and inner peace, as Divine and holy beings.

That's why I wrote this book. I want to help make you aware of your gorgeous and Divine Spirit and teach you how to love and live your Divine nature—starting now. Connecting people to their Spirit is my greatest passion and personal joy, and is something I've been committed to doing for the past 35 years. The most exciting part of my mission and message is that learning to love yourself and live your Spirit is actually quite simple once you realize the truth. And the truth is: You are *not* the ego. You are Divine. You are holy. You are Spirit.

Once you make that connection, loving your inner Divine light and beginning to live your Spirit, everything comes alive in light and joy. Love and live your Spirit, and your life flows peacefully. Be enslaved to and follow your fearful ego, and it doesn't. It really *is* that simple.

The ten simple yet necessary steps to forge that connection and experience your truth, your authentic Spirit, lie within these pages. Because you're designed to be a joyful, peaceful, magical, and highly empowered holy being, you'll find that these guidelines bring out your natural best. They may even seem disarmingly simple. Don't let this deceive you. I share what I know in this book with confidence. These aren't just metaphysical theories, but are tried-and-true, grounded practices that will lead you directly back to *you:* the best, holiest, most delightful and delighted you, free of fear and filled with light. I don't ask that you believe me—I only ask that you give them a try and see for yourself.

And *enjoy.* . . .

How to Use This Book

I've laid this book out in ten simple steps. Each is composed of two parts: The first introduces you to an idea about how to love yourself, and the second describes a practical action you can take to strengthen your love of self and devotion to Spirit.

In the middle of the book, I've added an interlude called "The Heart of the Matter." This section introduces you to the four aspects of the heart of self-love—*openness, clarity, wisdom,* and *courage*—and shows you how to deepen your capacity to cherish yourself even more. These lessons will help you balance your heart and recognize which aspects of self-love you're strong in and which you need to pay more attention to.

You can approach these pages in any way you wish: a step at a time, a week at a time, a concept at a time, or a practice at a time, as your Spirit calls you. This book isn't laid out in any particular sequence, but simply suggests the necessary elements for freeing yourself from the fear and control of the ego, and connecting with the joy and light of the Divine.

It is my wish in writing this book that you enter into the greatest love affair you'll ever experience in this life: a love affair with your beautiful, Divine, authentic, holy Spirit. So if you're ready, so am I.

Let's begin. . . .

STEP 1

Recognize Your Spirit

Simple Lesson: Recognize Your Spirit

This step introduces you to who you really are: a Divine Spirit and Holy Child of God. It focuses on distinguishing your false self (your ego) from your true, authentic self (your Spirit) and aims to help you accept your holy and sacred nature. This new awareness becomes grounded in the breathing practice following the lesson, which frees you from the ego habit of negative self-judgment and fear and gives you access to the lightness of heart that comes with Spirit.

❀

The very first step toward loving yourself and living your Spirit is recognizing who you really are. So many of us have grown up believing that we're unacceptable, sinful—even contemptible—beings. We've often been told that we're somehow tainted, broken, and consequently, basically unlovable.

Whatever cultural, religious, or psychological reasons are behind this message, our acceptance of the
notion that we're unworthy comes from our tendency
to seek love from the outside. We've been led to believe
that we're only our ego or personality, and the one we
have is just not good enough. Along the way, we've also
been told—what feels like a billion times, from a billion
different people—that unless we do what others want us
to do, we don't deserve to be loved . . . and won't be.

In relentless ways, we've been indoctrinated to have
low self-esteem and to measure our worth and lovability
by our capacity to win approval. If we're good at winning it, we feel loved and lovable. If we aren't so good
at doing so, we feel *un*loved and *un*lovable. The trouble
is, no one can possibly earn enough approval to feel
securely loved for their entire life. Approval is much too
fickle for that.

Seeking love through our egos, from the outside in,
is a doomed prospect. Because our egos—which aren't
our true selves—can never be loved enough to feel satisfied, and because we can never control what's outside
of us consistently, we'll never succeed if we seek to love
ourselves in this way. Furthermore, having worked so
intimately with people for so many years, I venture to
suggest that on an intuitive, organic level, we know
this system won't work. Deep down, most of us realize
that we can't find adequate self-love through gaining
approval from others. We can only find it by appreciating and valuing ourselves from within, from a place that
goes deeper than ego or personality.

The key is recognizing that we're all Divine Spirit—
as beautiful, unique creations of God. The Holy Mother/
Father God breathed life into us all and delights in our
existence in every way. It is up to *us* to do the same.

Self-love starts with knowing that we are Spirit. We have bodies. We have personalities. We have histories, stories, and experiences. But we *are not* those things—we are Spirit. Our bodies, egos, intellects, and personalities are tools that our Spirit uses to express itself in our physical embodiment. They're useful. They color and influence our experience. They affect our outlook, behavior, responses, and choices. They make life interesting—but they're nevertheless only implements for our Spirit to use. They aren't who we are.

I say "our Spirit" because just as there's only one fire, there's only one Spirit. Just as the flames in a fireplace, a lighter, a furnace, a barbeque, and a forest fire are all expressions of one element, we, too, are all unique expressions of a single Spirit.

If that's true, and the One Divine Holy Spirit gives all of us life, then it leads us to conclude that there are no "others," no outsiders whose approval we must seek. There's just us. In other words, there's no other Spirit, separate from us, judging us. We're made of the same stuff, evolving and learning at different paces and in different ways, of course, but still the same.

If you look at yourself and at life through the lens of your ego, you'll feel isolated, ganged up on, alone, different, and not part of the crowd. If you look through the lens of Spirit, knowing we're all one, you'll always feel safe, secure, and loved.

Although you may have a less-than-stellar personality, a less-than-sharp intellect, and a less-than-"Hollywood" figure, you're nevertheless a gorgeous, beautiful, wondrous, miraculous manifestation of Spirit . . . for it is nothing short of a miracle when the Holy Spirit descends into your being with your first breath. The body is formed, but without that breath of life, that spark of Divine consciousness, there's no *you*.

You're Divine. You're made of light, love, and grace. You're holy, and your body and personality are the caretakers of this sacred presence. To house this Divinity in your being, in your physical self, is a gift and should be a pleasure. To accept your true nature is a huge, undeniable step toward self-love.

I shared this idea with a client of mine named Patty a few years ago. She was the only child of a tough, withholding single mother. She grew up in perpetual fear of her mom's disapproval and constant criticism. All of her life she was told, and felt, that she wasn't worth much. Seeking approval, nevertheless, and fighting off the plague of self-loathing that was projected on her at a young age, she was an exemplary person in every way: She was at the head of her class, a straight-A student, the neighborhood's best babysitter, the most consistent volunteer and fund-raiser at her church, and a reliable neighbor and good friend to all. Yet she didn't love herself. She didn't even *like* herself. She couldn't even imagine doing so.

To protect herself from the psychic assaults on her Spirit from her ego, she gained weight slowly over time. By the time she was 50, she was 100 pounds overweight and climbing—both in self-loathing and despair as well as in pounds.

That's when we met. She attended a workshop I was giving in Chicago (where I live), in which I suggested that she treat her Spirit like a sacred and beloved guest in her heart. That idea captured her imagination.

"Coming from the South," she said with a giggle, "I always prided myself on being the world's best hostess.

But when it came to hosting my Spirit, I was abominable and knew it. It was time to change, if for no other reason than that it was bad manners!"

She accepted the challenge on the spot and embraced her Spirit and began to honor it. She started to create a calm, peaceful atmosphere in her home. She monitored what she said about herself to others so as not to insult her Spirit. She prepared healthful, beautiful, fresh meals and took her time eating them so that her Spirit could enjoy them. She spoke to her Spirit with respect and affection and repeatedly thanked it for being in her heart, asking what she could do to make it feel more at home.

She stopped internally listening to the past negative feedback that had haunted her all her life and began to respect and honor her Spirit's voice instead.

Slowly things changed. The first thing she noticed was that she was sleeping better; and as she slept better, she ate better—most notably, consuming less sugar just to get through the day. As she ate better, she felt better, so she started to be more active. As she did so, she made new friends and dropped some weight. She also stopped smoking (another unloving act) and got a new job. A year and a half later, she met a new guy and got married—her first marriage at 53.

She's certain that she married because of her shift in identity. When she lived life beholden to her ego, she'd felt too unlovable to be close to anyone or let anyone get too close her. As soon as she started attending to her Spirit with respect and care, she opened up.

On her third date with the man who's now her husband, he said, "I just love your Spirit."

"So do I," she replied. "Finally, so do I."

Once you decide to recognize your Spirit, the next step is to *live* it. To do so is to honor and respect your most authentic Divine self, remembering who you really are and expressing it in the world. To live your Spirit is to rise above the pain and confusion of the human ego and travel through life as the Divine Being you're designed to be. It's your true identity—this is your purpose . . . this is the Divine plan. This is the only way.

Einstein said it best: "The intuitive mind is a sacred gift and the rational mind its faithful servant. We have created a society that honors the servant and has forgotten the gift."

This is why we fail to find success through the ego. This is why life, for many, is an endless drama and struggle—because we follow our inferior guide, the one that's defensive, unclear, poorly informed, confused, easily intimidated, self-absorbed, and fearful.

Furthermore, no matter how we cater to the ego (which it loves, by the way), it will never be other than what it is: a posturing, confused, defensive, insecure, needy, demanding dictator who basically holds us hostage and robs us of joy and peace.

To live your Spirit is simple: All you must do is detach from your ego and follow your heart. By adopting certain daily practices that are simple but honest expressions of *you*—such as listening to your inner voice, being flexible and changing direction if it's called for, keeping your heart open, and laughing throughout the day—you'll naturally raise the energetic frequency of your Spirit above that of ego. The more you resonate with the frequency or vibration of Spirit, the stronger the connection becomes. And the stronger it becomes, the clearer the direction your Spirit offers in your life.

When you begin to live your Spirit, the first thing you'll feel is its presence in your heart. It conveys an actual energetic sensation. For some, this is a subtle fluttering; for others, it's a warm, intense buzz. For some, it feels like relief, as though a missing piece to the puzzle has been found. For others, it "pings," "clicks," or "rings true." In all cases, the minute you raise your vibration enough to connect with your Spirit, you feel *real, genuine, authentic, whole,* and *satisfied.* The empty restlessness within you quiets down. The void fills up and physically you begin to relax and enjoy life.

As you strengthen this connection to Spirit, you'll experience even more distinctive shifts:

- Your belly will ease; you'll become more relaxed.

- Your defenses will drop and your heart will open up.

- Your breathing will deepen and tension in your body will begin to lift.

This is because as you return to wholeness, you start to feel safe. Because you're no longer compensating for missing guidance, or flying by the seat of your fearful pants, every cell in your body, every muscle, and every ligament begins to ease. Because Spirit is the life force, you'll also feel more youthful, optimistic, and alive.

Burt was only 63 years old, but due to the fear and anxiety his ego put him through, he felt and acted much older. When he came to see me, he was troubled by arthritis, back pain, and depression. He saw a therapist once a week and was on antidepressants and pain medication, yet he was barely able to move about freely, let alone possess the desire to do so. He spent a great deal of time alone in his home, feeling unloved and sorry for himself. His daughter suggested a session with me as a last resort to help him reengage with life, to which he agreed.

When we met, I could see that his fear and negative self-judgment, and not his physical ailments, were robbing him of his life force. I suggested to him that his Spirit was alive and well and that his fear was interfering with his life. To my surprise, he agreed.

"I know there's nothing really wrong with me," he admitted. "Or at least nothing that can't be fixed if I allow it. I just don't know what to live for if I do get better. I feel so unhappy and unfulfilled all the time, and I don't know how to get free of this feeling. I feel like such a failure."

I encouraged him to keep working with his doctors, but, in addition, to consider his Spirit and start to love and follow it. This was a novel idea to him.

"Hmm . . ." he considered. "My Spirit, you say? I think we parted ways long ago."

"Why?" I asked.

"I don't know," he replied. "I guess it just seemed easier to ignore it than to try to follow it . . . thought it was too late, I suppose."

"And if you were to reverse that idea now and express your Spirit after all, what would you do?" I inquired.

"I'd pick up my guitar, write some songs, and sing a little," he answered without a moment's hesitation, as if he'd already been contemplating that question. "But then again, I'm too old for that," he continued.

"Maybe," I answered. "But then again, it may be the fountain of youth and bring vitality back into your bones. Did you ever consider that?"

When he heard this, he smirked, but I could tell that he was listening nevertheless. He was quiet for a long while, and then he said, "Maybe you're right. It *feels* right." He got up, stretched, and announced: "I think I got what I needed to hear. Thank you very much." Then he left.

Six months later I received a package in the mail from Burt. In it was a letter that read: "I still have a little back pain from time to time, but I'm not depressed anymore and I'm getting around some. By the way, I thought you might like to hear a few songs I wrote. Instead of living the blues, I started *singing* the blues, as you suggested, and I must admit I do feel a whole lot better now. So thank you."

As you connect more with your Spirit, you'll be less entranced by the fearful running dialogue of your ego and begin to hear life's song more deeply. You'll become more capable of listening to and actually absorbing messages from others and the world around you. You'll not only hear the content; you'll begin to register the *intent* behind communication, too.

As you continue to strengthen your relationship with your Spirit, the mental chatter of your ego will quiet down. The suspicions, insecurities, second-guessing, defensive dialogues, and ruminating over your less-than-successful past will begin to decrease. And with this new-found quiet, your attention will be drawn to the sound, feeling, and vibration of your inner voice. You'll begin to hear your guidance. Much like a GPS (Global Positioning System) in a car that can guide you efficiently from point A to point B, your inner radar will kick in and start to direct you toward your deepest goals.

My client Joseph connected to his Spirit and found that everything fell into place. As the only son in his family, Joseph felt obliged to work in his father's real estate business. For more than 15 years he managed apartments instead of following his secret dream of becoming a chef. Fear of financial insecurity and of letting down his father caused him to abandon his Spirit and get stuck in a rut of ego control. One day, after feeling unbearably frustrated over his lackluster life, he spontaneously enrolled in a cooking school at night. Following his Spirit rewarded him immediately: The very first week he met a wonderfully supportive woman who made him laugh, encouraged him, and fell in love with him. With her help, he started to return to his authentic self.

While in school, he also met another frustrated student who wanted to change his course as well. By the time the first year ended, the two had decided to explore the idea of opening a restaurant together. No sooner had Joseph made this decision than his father announced he was retiring and asked Joseph if he wanted to carry on the business or quit. Scared of disappointing his father but more scared of disappointing himself, Joseph finally admitted that he wanted to quit the business and open his own restaurant instead.

He was shocked by his father's reaction. Not only was he supportive, but he said he'd be willing to invest in the business and help them find a location. Once Joseph decided to live his Spirit, it seemed as if, by magic, his father came on board as well.

That's how it works: Once you choose to love yourself and align with your Spirit, life aligns with *you*. Obstacles give way to openings, and struggle turns to support.

You begin to experience what I refer to as "catching the wave." Others have called it "getting into the flow" or my favorite, "entering a state of grace." Whatever you call it, it feels great. You no longer have to agonize over, or try to control, life. You just show up and life carries you to greater and greater experiences.

This all sounds incredible, doesn't it? Well, as one who lives this way, I can assure you that it is. Again, it isn't difficult. All that's required is that you choose to live as a Divine Being and follow your Spirit as opposed to living as an ego-bound being, following your fears. Only the decision is difficult. Once you make it, the rest gets easier and easier and easier.

Simple Practice: Breathe

Breath is essential to living and loving your Spirit. In fact, your breath *is* your Spirit. The air you take in gives you life. To breathe deeply is to claim your Spirit and bring it into every cell of your body.

One of the first things that occurs when you disconnect from your Spirit and get entangled in the drama and confusion of the false ego self is that you stop breathing deeply. You tend to breathe shallowly instead, and even occasionally to hold your breath altogether. When your body doesn't get adequate oxygen, it goes more deeply into fear and anxiety, thus creating a vicious cycle of self-debilitating negativity. So to love your Spirit—to live your Spirit—you must *breathe*.

There are several ways to do so that instantly align you with your Divine Spirit and raise your vibration:

1. The first is to breathe in deeply through your nose and then open your mouth, relax the back of your throat, and release the sound "Ahh" as you exhale. Practice this several times right now and notice the change in your vibration. While you do, place your hand over your heart and feel its vibration as your breath releases. This kind of breathing isn't unusual—we all do it naturally. It's called a "sigh." When we sigh, we get out of our heads and our false ego selves and reconnect to Spirit. It's a natural reflex to keep us true to our higher self.

Breathing in this way frees us immediately from being stuck in our negative-ego, fear-based vicious-thought cycles and stabilizes us in a higher, loving, authentic vibration. It's a self-loving, self-affirming technique that I recommend doing as often as possible throughout the day.

I laughingly refer to this breathing technique as a "get out of jail free" tool of self-care, as it immediately releases us from the prison of our mental addictions and sufferings. The more deeply we breathe, the calmer, clearer, and more peaceful we become.

A doctor once told me that a person can't breathe deeply and worry at the same time—it's biologically impossible. A deep breath interrupts and dissipates worry waves. I can't say for certain that this is universally true, but I *can* say that it is true for me. When I breathe in through the nose and slowly out through the mouth with an "Ahh . . ." I can't feel anxious about anything. I can only feel relaxation, easing of tension, and relief. It's great!

Try it yourself and see if *you* can worry and breathe at the same time. Of course, you can worry between breaths if you'd like, but if you breathe consistently, even that becomes more and more difficult to do.

2. Another breathing technique that calms the mind and raises your vibration instantly to the frequency of Spirit is called "The Breath of Fire." This practice is useful when your ego mind has gotten so knotted up in a tangle of worry that you can't seem to break free or connect with your Spirit, no matter what you do.

Stand with your legs slightly apart and bent a little at the knees, then take in the deepest breath you can and quickly thump your chest with your fist in the area of your heart, releasing a loud, resounding "Ha!" To get the best results, make certain you're free to be as loud as you can when you do this thump on the heart. The "Ha!" is the equivalent of a lifeguard's whistle alerting: "Everybody out of the pool now!" It energetically breaks up and dispels any negative frequencies that have gotten hold of you and restores your vibration to your authentic, Divine frequency.

This breathing technique can be a little startling to you and anyone around you. That's the point. It startles your ego mind into release and calls your Spirit into your body. It acts as a reset button on your energy patterns.

After you take your breath, thump your chest, and expel an emphatic "Ha!" slowly breathe in and then listen. In your head you'll hear beautiful, glorious silence— the peace and quiet of Divine mind. This exercise, done two or three times a day, clears your energy of all negativity and quiets the brain. It kicks your ego out of the driver's seat and puts your Spirit back in control.

3. Another breathing suggestion is that throughout the day—and especially when under stress—you step away from whatever you're doing and take a "breather": literally a break to simply breathe deeply for five minutes and realign your consciousness with your Spirit.

Breathers aren't unnecessary indulgences. Rather, they are essential self-loving time-outs we all need throughout the day. The entire world would be a whole lot better off if everyone took a few more of them. The breath we're taking connects us to all of life. We all share it; therefore, we're all interconnected.

Not only is taking a breather an enormously *self-loving* choice, it's a loving choice for the entire human race. Every one of us who aligns with the vibration of Spirit influences those around us to do so. It's contagious—in a good way.

4. Finally, try to "share a breath." By this I mean breathe in unison with another . . . falling, if possible, into a common breathing pattern for several minutes.

The breath is our common bond, the great Divine equalizer. When you share a breath with another, you automatically remove any obstacles, barriers, fears, and judgments that exist between you. It's impossible to feel threatened, unsafe, unworthy, or disconnected when you breathe in unison.

This tool doesn't necessarily change how you feel about one another on a mental level. Your ego mind may still want to hold on to its resentments, judgments, and negative feelings. Yet, if you breathe in unison with someone, the vibration between you begins to harmonize and resonate on a higher frequency. This softens your heart and brings you to Divine mind, where there's no place for conflict.

I recently found myself in a situation where I needed to share a breath with another to bring peace. I'm glad to say that it *does* work.

Our family was vacationing in Paris, where I'd rented an apartment for a week during the summer. It was a trip that I'd dreamed of, planned, and looked forward to for more than a year. Just before we left, my younger daughter, Sabrina, asked me if two of her newfound friends could stay with us for two days in our apartment as they backpacked across Europe.

Remembering my own backpacking days and how grateful I was for any kindness extended my way as a young traveler, I readily agreed and said that they could sleep on the sofas. In fact, I thought that their presence would add to the festivities. Their visit, however, was full of surprises.

First, the two showed up earlier than planned, in the middle of the night on the very first day we arrived. The next surprise was greater: They planned to stay six nights, not the two I'd agreed to—in other words, for the entire vacation. Again, this took a mental adjustment, but I was willing to be a good sport. After all, my daughters enjoyed the company and were having a nice time, which had been my intent for the vacation.

Then the challenges began. Neither of the guests had any money, so they ate with us every day—breakfast, lunch, and dinner. Even this didn't bother me because we had plenty to share. What *did* bother me, however, were the manners of one of the travelers.

While the young man was friendly, pleasant, helpful, and a joy to be around, his traveling companion was quite the opposite. She was unhelpful, didn't pick up after herself, and never offered to aid in the preparation of meals or clean up afterward, even though everything was obviously a team effort all the way. She ate our food; drank our wine; monopolized the one computer in the house; scattered her things all over the living room; and chain-smoked on the balcony, leaving mounds and mounds of cigarette butts in several ashtrays for others to empty. This was in spite of my repeated—at first gentle, then increasingly firm—requests that she chip in, help out, clean up, and be a good guest.

Needless to say, after three days my ego mind went into overdrive with indignation. How dare she barge in on my vacation, help herself to my things, leave me to clean up her mess, and show no appreciation at all?! My resentment moved in like a dark gray cloud of pollution and began to rob me of any and all pleasure in being on my vacation. I was so consumed with righteous victimization that I was miserable beyond belief. I swore she knew that she was loathsome to be around but didn't care. I would have asked her to leave, but my daughters protested, as they enjoyed the other guest completely and the two were a pair. My only recourse was to get out of my ego mind and get back to Divine Spirit. But how—especially since my ego couldn't stand to be in her presence?

Then one night I got a break. There was a funny show in English on television that drew us all in. We sat there in the same room, watching quietly, when I suddenly decided to share a breath with her for a while.

As I did so, the first thing I noticed was that she didn't breathe very deeply, which made me aware of how fearful she was, not just about us, but about life in general. As I continued to breathe with her, I also noticed how unaware one becomes with so little breath. Between the shallow breaths and the cigarettes, she was most likely nearly unconscious of her surroundings. No wonder she contributed so little—she just didn't see enough to offer. I also realized what chaos her ego brain was in. Shallow, rapid breathing creates turmoil in the body. With so much chaos inside, it simply spilled over into her environment. That explained why she was such a pigpen.

By the time the show was over, breathing with her put me back into Divine mind. My heart opened to her, and I realized that she was a courageous girl to create this adventure for herself, and although she was a terrible guest, it was only because she was trying to manage her own fears. I looked at her and let out an easy "Ahh" and thumped my chest. Then I surprised everyone by shouting "Ha!" This snapped me out of the negative spell I'd been under and lifted my Spirit. I gave her a spontaneous hug, which she didn't understand.

The pair left the next morning, two days early.

STEP 2

Welcome Your Spirit

Simple Lesson: Welcome Your Spirit

This step asks you to welcome your Spirit and invite it fully into your life. The practice that follows guides you to create a loving and receptive home for it in your body. With this new awareness, you'll come to view your physical self as your faithful ally and friend and become happily grounded in your own skin.

❋

Getting over yourself—your false ego self—is the first step toward living a blessed, charmed, peaceful life. But that's not enough. Once you *dis*connect from your false self, your ego, it's important to actively *connect* with your authentic, Divine self—your Spirit.

Begin by accepting that you have a beautiful, blessed, gorgeous, holy force that lives in the center of your heart and gives you life: a brilliant flame of Divine love. It's a force that we all have, we all share, and we all depend on for our existence. In other words, this holy spark of life is the essence of your authentic self as a Divine Being. While the ego is finite and dies with your body, your Spirit is infinite and lives on without physical limitations. Your Spirit after death simply returns to the great Creator, the Holy Mother/Father God, and resumes being the light it is made of.

A miracle happens when you stop believing that you are your ego self and start connecting to your Spirit—when you stop controlling and fearing life and start enjoying it. This is because when you're in Spirit, you align with Divine mind. You become one with God. And as my mother always said, "When God is with you, no one is against you, because nothing is greater than God."

Another reason why life becomes instantly better when you connect with your authentic self, the Divine Spirit within, is that you join with all else that's Divine, such as beauty, harmony, and our greatest of all desires, peace. In Divine mind, there's no war, sickness, poverty, combativeness, insecurity, fear, anger, or anything else that the ego mind is so addicted to and injured by. Instead, all is peaceful all the time.

To merge with Divine mind, identify with being the holy, sacred Spirit that you are. Of course, your ego mind will scoff at the very notion by saying, *Who do you think you are?* or *That's ridiculous.* It doesn't want you to know that you're Spirit—at least not without a fight, anyway— because as soon as you acknowledge that you are, it loses power. To claim your Spirit automatically displaces your ego and pushes it out of the job of running (and *ruining*) your life. Naturally, it doesn't want this to happen.

The paradox, however, is that when the ego mind is displaced by your Spirit, it actually relaxes and begins to enjoy life, because it's in its natural right place once again: following and supporting your Spirit, not fighting against it.

Years ago, when I was around ten years old, a gentleman came to our house to speak to my mother, who was an artist and portrait painter. Based on her reputation, he asked her if she would be willing to paint a portrait of the family of a well-known guru from India who was visiting at the time. Before she agreed, he told my mom that she'd have to prepare herself because the guru's presence was very holy, and in order to receive him, she—and all of us—would have to be in the right, high vibration. Checking out the vibes in the household, he gave us the basic okay but said that we'd need to ready ourselves, nevertheless.

We were required to clean the house, use special incense, pray, groom ourselves, put on our best clothes, and serve special teas and fruits. As we readied everything, I begrudgingly asked my mother if all of this was truly necessary. Why was he so important? She said that it *was* necessary, but not for the reasons I thought. She explained that it wasn't so much that he was special or holy or more important than us in any way—it was just that he *remembered* how holy he was. He recalled that he was a child of God and treated himself with the love and respect we all deserve. He served as a role model to remind us that we are holy and deserve the highest level of reverence because everyone's Spirit is worthy of that.

She emphasized the need to be mindful of our Spirit and its holiness, but not to confuse the Spirit with the ego.

"How do you know the difference?" I asked. "How can you tell? It seems to me they're easy to mix up."

"It's not hard to distinguish ego from Spirit," she answered. "When you're connected to Spirit, you feel as though you're a part of life and your heart opens to everyone. When you're tied to your ego, however, you want to pull away. You separate yourself from others. You adopt a me-against-you attitude and close your heart.

"An easier way to discern ego from Spirit is to check in with your vibes. When you connect with your Spirit, you feel good, positive, self-loving vibes. When you connect to your ego, you feel irritable, critical, depressed, and tired vibes. Simple!"

Our conversation left a big impression on me. We should all treat our Spirit as a sacred guest and receive it with the same attention and care we would extend a special visitor.

Imagine your Spirit as a sacred guest taking up residence in your life. If this were the case, how would you prepare to receive your company?

Imagine doing the very things for your Spirit that you would do for someone you loved, even adored: Invite it into a calm space in your body. Relax and greet it with your most gracious smile and welcoming attitude. Make it feel at home. Imagine speaking to your Spirit with kindness, affection . . . even reverence, as it's a holy essence.

Your Spirit is a sacred and holy part of your life. It's only appropriate that you prepare for and host it to the best of your abilities. This means creating a loving, grounded home for your Spirit to reside in by taking care of your body. Just as you would probably not want an important visitor to come into your home if it were messy, chaotic, or toxic, neither should you impose this kind of disrespect and disarray onto your Spirit.

Give your Spirit a healthy, happy home to dwell in. This means, among other things, offering it a body that's properly fed, well rested, somewhat exercised, clean, and appreciated. That certainly is far more inviting to it than one that's overstuffed with bad foods or starved altogether; or that's exhausted, full of toxic substances, lethargic, and ignored. In fact, if the environment of your body becomes too unhealthy, your Spirit leaves because the vibration is too low. It literally steps out of your physical self, seeking to get away from the disaster and dissonance inside.

If a person's Spirit has departed from his or her body, it leaves nothing but a fearful, controlling ego to run the show in its place. If the Spirit has vacated, you'll see no light in the individual's eyes—no spark, no fire, and no luminescence. When you look into them, you'll only perceive a dull emptiness, as if no one is home.

Sadly, neglect isn't the only reason the Spirit steps out of the body. Trauma, abuse, physical injury, self-loathing, extreme anger, or fear also can dislodge it. Fortunately, when the Spirit steps out, it doesn't go far—it simply moves outside the physical body yet remains connected by what metaphysicians call the *silver cord* above it. The Spirit continues to be energetically connected to you but isn't embodied. This leaves you weak, and easily influenced by lower vibrations.

Don't worry if you feel that yours has left your body. It can happen to any of us from time to time if we're not aware of, and loving toward, the Spirit. It departs due to long exposure to intense negative vibration, such as when you get into an angry argument with another, when you abuse drugs or alcohol, or when you experience or perpetrate severe violence. Your Spirit also leaves if you're on a path that doesn't serve you, which is what happened to one of my clients.

A young woman came to me for a consultation not long ago. When I looked into her eyes, it was clear that her Spirit wasn't at home. Her eyes were dull, her energy was low, and there wasn't an ounce of enthusiasm or joy to be found in her being. She loathed her job as a middle-school counselor for behaviorally challenged adolescents and had wanted to quit for more than two years. Yet the fear of lacking income kept her going to the job, day after day—at least, it kept her *body* going. Her Spirit had left and wasn't involved in any part of that decision, only her ego.

When I suggested that she quit and follow her Spirit to where it wanted to be, which was working as an intuitive guide and counselor, her ego immediately rejected the idea, saying that if she did that, she wouldn't make it. She didn't register that without her Spirit, she wasn't surviving well already, nor was she doing the kids at school much good, either—a fact I pointed out to her. The entire vibration of the situation wasn't good for her, and she suffered as a result of continuing to go against the grain of her Spirit.

Listening to me, my client had to admit that the vibration of the job was toxic for her. It was never a comfortable fit, and she'd never liked being there. In fact, she said she hated it, a clear sign that her Spirit had left. The Spirit never "hates" a thing, only the controlling ego does.

As we spoke, she actually started to entertain the idea of quitting and perhaps working at a local spiritual bookstore, both as a salesperson and a counselor. Just the thought of this possibility lured her Spirit back in.

Her eyes lit up, her smile returned, and she sighed with relief.

I wasn't the only one who noticed. *She* felt it, too. "Oh my goodness!" she exclaimed. "That would be so wonderful . . . I feel better just thinking about it."

Evidently, she began to honor the need for her Spirit to be in a better vibration than she was in at her school job, because I heard that she did quit and was teaching and doing spiritual counseling through the bookstore, just as we'd talked about.

❀

The minute you decide to welcome your Spirit—to place loving attention on it; to give priority to it; to treat it as a holy, sacred guest in your heart; and to honor it and put it in a positive atmosphere—you raise the vibration of your body and it snaps right back in. No problem.

Remember that everything in this universe ultimately comes down to vibration, which is either positive, kind, loving, appreciative, respectful, harmonious, and life affirming (the frequency of God mind) or dissonant, negative, demoralizing, guilt tripping, judgmental, critical, hostile, and life destroying (the frequency of ego mind).

To be critical, hostile, and shaming toward your authentic self is the equivalent of hurling insults and garbage at your holy guest in residence. It's life destroying and patently unacceptable to your Spirit. You wouldn't treat an invited human guest in this way, so why would you ever agree to do this to your Divine Spirit?

You get my point. *So do not attack yourself anymore,* because it is hurtful to the Spirit. Instead, welcome, embrace, and honor it fully. It's a sacred guest residing in your heart. The more you treat it so, the more beautiful your life will become.

Simple Practice: Love Your Body

Probably the thing we love the least about ourselves is our physical bodies. Everyone, and I do mean *everyone,* has been bombarded with crazy ideas about what constitutes a lovable physical body; and no one, and I do mean *no one,* has that body. This is because "that body"—the externally perfect, gorgeous, lean, strong, sexy, flawless body—is not a human one. It's a fiction of the media and doesn't exist . . . not among human beings. And even if it *seems* to exist, as in the case of some Hollywood stars, it either doesn't for long (bodies change and age) or it comes at such a price of fear, control, obsession, and addiction that although the outside may temporarily look terrific, the inside is usually a disaster.

Our obsession with our bodies is rooted in the notion that if we look good (whatever that means), we have far greater chances of being loved and feeling secure. The problem with this notion is twofold: (1) Feeling loved in this way is based on winning other people's approval, which we know the ego can never get enough of; and (2) the notion of what is beautiful is very subjective and changeable, so we'll never get it "right," even if we try.

For example, one year the "look" is to have long straight hair; the next, it's to have short curly hair. One year it's to be heroin-chic thin; the next, it's to be muscular and lean. One season men need facial hair to be considered "cool" or acceptable; the next, they should be clean shaven with shoulder-length hair. And that's only in the Western world. I just read an article about how extreme obesity in young women is considered to be supreme beauty among men in Mauritania, so girls are fattened like geese, forced to eat to pile on the pounds so that they're attractive bride material. Some are so overweight that they can't even walk, yet these are considered pearls of great price there.

This standard of beauty is ridiculous—not to mention downright ignorant—and is abusive to these women. To subscribe to it is insanity . . . but it's no less toxic or absurd than our doing hothouse yoga in 150-degree rooms on an empty stomach. Don't you think, in the name of self-love, it's time to stop and ask ourselves—especially when it comes to our bodies: "What the heck are we doing—and why?"?

If we actually believe that looking a certain contrived way physically is the key to self-love, we've completely disconnected from our Spirit. Over the years I've counseled a number of actresses and models, all considered gorgeous. Underneath their perfectly coiffed, manicured, cellulite-free, abs-of-steel bodies, however, are some of the most unhappy, ego-obsessed, miserably self-loathing, spiritless people I've ever encountered. Their lives have been reduced to gyms, beauty salons, and mirrors; and there's room for little else. It's sad and boring and wastefully joyless! And it's not self-loving at all . . . it's ego-controlling, and the control is being reinforced by popular opinion, which is rooted in absolute fear, terror of rejection, and misery. So what kind of reward is that?

Regardless of how we look, it's how we feel in our own skin that matters. And until we consider our bodies

to be our friends and our faithful and devoted servants—
recognizing that they, too, are sacred and holy creations,
just as our Spirit is—we can't feel good or ever be at
peace.

Treat your body as your friend, because it *is:* It tirelessly serves you—in spite of your attitude toward it—
and allows you to serve your Spirit and support your life
with love. It's a miraculous vessel that takes quite a bit of
abuse, while still working for you every day.

To love yourself, you must love your body as well—it
comes as a package deal. No matter what kind of body
you ended up with, it's the only one you have, so you
must live with it whether you want to or not. Realize
how important your physical self is to your life's journey
—not for the approval it wins from others, but for the
service it provides your Spirit. It's your vessel, your car-
rier, your means of experiencing life. Like a car that gets
you from point A to point B, it's your mode of transpor-
tation on Earth and will work much better for you if you
treat it with a little respect and care.

There are a lot of commonsense reasons to love your
body, topped by the fact that if you don't, sooner or later
the neglect and rejection will come back to haunt you
in the form of sickness, fatigue, depression, or some sort
of pain. So first and foremost, it's a practical choice to
befriend your body. And the easiest way to begin is to
appreciate it from the inside out. Stop obsessing or worrying about how it looks (because, after all, unless you're
in front of a mirror, you aren't scrutinizing it anyway),
and start paying attention to how it *feels*. Especially pay
attention to what makes it feel *better.*

One thing that I know will make it feel better is kind
words. The body is a sensitive, vibrationally responsive

vessel. Kind words have a highly positive physical effect on you, while harsh criticisms—voiced or internalized—have a stressful impact. So talk to yourself in a loving way.

Years ago when my daughter Sabrina was only four years old, my husband, Patrick, lost his patience with her because she was being uncooperative, and he lashed out at her with some harsh words. Shocked, she stopped and took in what he said, sitting silently for a moment. Finally, she responded, "Dad, that's no way to talk to my Spirit, and my belly feels bad when you say that! Say you're sorry now so my belly feels better."

Surprised, but realizing Sabrina was being absolutely honest about the impact of his words on her stomach, Patrick immediately apologized. She was quiet for another minute, absorbing what he said. Then she remarked, "Okay, my belly's better now."

This was a clear reminder to all of us that the human body is sensitive and responds to what it's told. When you tell it harsh things, it feels bad. Magically (or so it seems), when you tell it loving things, it feels—guess what?—better.

Our habit of negative self-talk is so entrenched within us that we're not even aware of it. When listening to people talk about their bodies, the words I hear most often are *I hate:* "I hate my hair, thighs, balding head, waistline, feet, crooked teeth, freckles, wrinkles," and so on. Would you say that to your worst enemy, let alone to a friend who works tirelessly to transport you around? Of course not. Yet the pattern is there.

To break this habit, I believe we need lessons in, or at least reminders of, how to speak to ourselves. Make a list that reads: *"When I talk to myself, here's what I need to say. . . ."* Then write down as many loving, affirming statements as you can think of and would want to share with your best friend. Start from the inside out, and focus on what's within more than the outside.

For example:

- *You are so faithful, body. Thank you for getting up and going every day.*

- *You are such a good friend. Thanks for being reliable.*

- *You are intelligent, creative, and funny. I know that I can count on you.*

- *You are hearty, resilient, and powerful. I appreciate all you do for me.*

- *You are so cute/handsome.*

- *You are great.*

At the same time make a list of kind words you can say to your Spirit, such as:

- *I am glad that you are present.*
- *I hope that you are comfortable.*
- *Thank you for your grace.*
- *It is so wonderful to feel your grace.*
- *I love you.*

Type up this list and post it prominently in your field of vision. Turn it into a screen saver on your computer. Print it out and put it on your dashboard. Place a copy in your wallet. Stick it on every mirror in the house so that each time you look at yourself you have kind words for yourself. You can even call your cell phone and leave your list as a message.

To view yourself, and especially your body, with criticism is very physically damaging. Ancient cultures and Eastern belief systems recognized this and even created amulets to ward off "the evil eye."

In the name of self-love and love for your body, don't cast the evil eye—or as children rightfully call it, "the stink eye"—onto your body . . . ever. Shower light, love, and affection onto it instead. Speak kindly to your body if for no other reason than because it's basic manners to treat a friend with respect.

Another way to honor your physical self is to take care of it. Twenty-five years ago my mother gave my father the gift of a Cadillac Seville for their silver wedding anniversary. She knew that he wanted one and had saved for it for years. It was a beautiful, grand car and more glamorous than any he'd ever owned before. He treasured that vehicle: He washed and buffed it weekly. He changed the oil religiously, swept it out, covered the seats with protective covers, and most of all, spoke to and of it with appreciation. He cherished his gift and took great and loving care of it. Consequently, it drove and drove and drove. Outside of regular maintenance, the car never needed a thing—it ran like a dream.

I'm not suggesting that our human bodies are literally cars, but I do know that if we gave them half the care we tend to give other things, like our automobiles, we might succeed in feeling good in our own skin.

Start with the basics. All human bodies need lots of water, grains, greens, and protein. It's also a known fact that they're healthier if fed an alkaline diet, which consists of grains, greens, and nonanimal proteins. So to keep yours running well, eat more alkaline foods than acidic ones. To find out which are which, go on the Internet and search for "alkaline foods" and "acidic foods." If you primarily eat from the alkaline list, you'll feel better than if you don't.

Next, move a little. Movement makes the body happy, and a happy body helps feed a happy Spirit. Stand up, stretch, bend, walk, and wiggle. Move every hour or two, if only a little. It keeps the engine of the heart, lungs, and digestive system running well.

People ask me all the time how to get their weight or health under control. The answer is simple: Listen to your body (which is much easier to do if you speak nicely to it), and respect how you feel. Notice how your choices affect your physical being—not just in the moment, but in a few hours, or the next day. Make the ones that allow your body to feel good.

For example, I notice that even though I enjoy French bread and cheese, if I eat more than a little, I get very congested and can't breathe well soon after. When this happens, I don't sleep as soundly and don't feel good the next day. So I listen to my body and eat bread and cheese sparingly.

My husband loves a nice glass of wine or a beer, but his body doesn't. It leaves him feeling moody, unmotivated, and tired. He listened to this and stopped drinking because he didn't feel good afterward.

To listen to *your* body and respect how it feels is a powerful act of self-love. But be careful not to impose your own do's and don'ts on others. What is self-loving for your body isn't the same for *all* bodies.

Last year I was visiting my parents in Denver, and we decided to go out to eat. After dinner, the waiter came over and offered dessert, specifically the house specialty: warm chocolate cake with vanilla ice cream and caramel sauce.

My mother listened intently, then said, "My goodness, that sounds delicious, and I'm sure it is. But I love myself, and I know that if I eat it, I won't feel good later, so I'm going to say no and pass."

The waiter, surprised by her self-loving comment, said, "Well, who can argue with that? Okay."

Just then my dad piped up: "I love myself, too, so I'm going to say yes!" Then we all laughed out loud.

While the waiter set off to bring the dessert, I thought about what they both said. It was true that sweets didn't agree with my mom, who tends to be hypoglycemic, but they rarely if ever bothered my father. They both made the right choice. When the dessert came, I—who am learning to love *myself* better—said, "I love myself, too," and took only three bites. We all went home self-lovingly satisfied.

❁

When well cared for and cherished, your body becomes your best intuitive feedback system. It can warn you of danger through a gut feeling, the hair on the back of your neck standing up, or chills running up and down your arms. It can also register excitement through warmth in your throat, butterflies in your stomach, or lightness of heart. It's your best intuitive guide and will steadfastly get you *beyond* where you're going and toward the best possible circumstances at all times.

The more we love and care for our bodies, the more in tune we become with them.

❀   ❀   ❀

STEP 3

Know Your Spirit

Simple Lesson: Know Your Spirit

This step focuses on helping you better recognize how Spirit expresses itself through your individual personality. The practice that follows instills in you your Divine right to be happy and will stop your ego from robbing you of joy. As you embrace this new awareness, you'll no longer wait for happiness to find you—you'll <u>choose</u> it and will draw healthy and protective boundaries around your Spirit and your natural joy.

❁

Not only is it important to create an appropriate atmosphere in which your Spirit can reside, it's also important to become familiar with your Spirit itself. Notice the nature of yours in particular and what it likes . . . or better yet, *loves.*

When I ask my students or clients to tell me about their Spirit and what it's like and what it loves, I receive many blank stares and looks of confusion. "I don't *know* what my Spirit is like," I hear. "I've never thought about it before." And more explicitly, "What lets me know what my Spirit is like, let alone what it loves? I have no idea!"

Never fear—to discover what your Spirit is like is simple. It's the part of you that is light, happy, creative, and kind . . . the part of you that's present, lives in the moment, and laughs easily. It's the aspect of your nature that's tolerant, forgiving, easygoing, and confident. It is also the side of you that's enthusiastic and generous. Don't panic if you can't find or feel your Spirit within these descriptions. Even if your Spirit is hiding from you, as long as you're alive, so is *it*.

To identify your Spirit, know that in addition to these universal qualities, every Spirit possesses unique personal attributes as well. Some are feisty and rambunctious—I know mine is. Others—like my older daughter's or my father's, for example—are calmer, more laid-back, and subdued.

Some Spirits are grounded and practical and patient. These Spirits are *earthy* in temperament. Others are sensitive and empathic and compassionate—they're *watery*. Some Spirits are talkative, quick on their feet, and fiercely energetic. These are *fiery* Spirits. And some are wise—they take the long view and see the Big Picture. They are *airy* Spirits. From hearing these descriptions, are you able to better discern what kind of temperament *your* Spirit has?

This may be the first time you've considered this question, but once you begin to ponder it, your Spirit will reveal itself to you more and more.

To help you recognize and get to know your Spirit more intimately, look over the following short list of other typical Spirit characteristics to see which ones you can relate to:

— If you are an **earthy** Spirit, you tend to be:

- Solid
- Consistent
- Grounded
- Calm
- Slow to react
- Patient
- Affectionate

— If you are a **watery** Spirit, you tend to be:

- Sensitive
- Compassionate
- Empathic
- Emotional
- Nurturing
- Encouraging
- Moody

— If you are a **fiery** Spirit, you tend to be:

- Expressive
- Assertive
- Reactive
- Decisive
- Impulsive
- Confident
- Communicative

— If you are an **airy** Spirit, you tend to be:

- Global in perspective
- Objective
- Curious
- Resourceful
- Inventive

These, of course, are very generic descriptions, and it's not unusual for a Spirit to have some combination of the preceding characteristics—that is, you can be both a watery and an earthy Spirit at the same time. As Divine Beings, we draw from all aspects of conscious expression and often blend our Divine traits.

Another way to deeply appreciate and understand your Spirit is to identify what you love. What engages you so completely that you step away from all sense of time and space and simply enjoy the now? What thrills, delights, consumes, mesmerizes, and moves you? The answers to these questions tell you a lot about your Spirit. Write your responses down. Make a quick list of all the things you love and you'll get a solid sense of your unique Spirit and how it best wants to express itself.

For example, I love to travel—especially to exotic cities such as Marrakech, Jaipur, and Cairo. While there, I feel timeless, fascinated by the beauty and mystery these places hold.

I also love to shop, not necessarily to buy, but rather to fill my senses with all the creativity and invention I see in the various stores. I love the color, lighting, texture, smell, and taste of beautiful things. I can shop all day and not get even a bit tired.

I love to cuddle in bed with my (now-grown) daughters and watch reruns of our favorite TV shows while painting our toenails and sharing stories during commercials. No matter how tired I am after a busy day, I can spend hours sharing and laughing with my daughters before I even have the slightest desire to drift off to sleep.

I love biking with my husband, Patrick, and trying to keep up with him as he tears through the forest preserve near our home in Chicago. I love how my heart beats so fast that I think it's going to pop out of my chest as I ride, and the high I feel after we're done. I can ride for hours without getting tired, even if I'm exhausted when I start out.

Every time I open a workshop, I ask my students to share with each other what they love as a way to beckon their Spirits to wake up. No matter how subdued the group may be when we begin, in five short minutes the room is abuzz with energy and vitality as everyone describes what they love. I hear bursts of laughter and shared enthusiasm among strangers within seconds. The Spirit is not only *your* source of joy; sharing its loves is a source of joy for all. Every time I teach, I'm amazed by how quickly a roomful of shy, withholding people transforms into a group of what feels like old friends by simply announcing what their Spirits love.

Try it and you'll see what I mean. Take a sheet of paper, right now if possible, and begin. The less you think and the more quickly you write, the better. Jot down everything you love. Give this exercise no more than five minutes at the most. Anything more than that and your ego takes over. Then study your list. It will give you great insight into your Spirit's unique temperament and energy.

Here's a sample list:

I love . . .

- Family
- Rock music
- Dancing
- Fresh flowers
- Beautiful dresses
- Great shoes
- Dinner parties
- Good pillows
- Passports

- French bread and cheese
- Paris, travel, and friends
- Telling stories
- Singing
- Teaching
- Praying
- Sleeping
- Laughing

Of course, your list may not cite all that you love, but it jump-starts a relatively good and clear beginning. The above lists some of my core loves, which are the food and fuel of my Spirit—the things that strengthen and feed my authentic self. If I engage or connect with the items on this list, I feel instantly happy and peaceful, which tells me that I'm connected to my Spirit and Divine mind. I can also tell by the list that I'm a fiery, airy Spirit who loves comfort, adventure, and inspiring others.

Now look over *your* list. It will reveal intriguing insights to you as well. Once it's written out, run it by a good friend and ask the other person if there's anything you've overlooked. Then run it by a family member or someone who has known you your entire life. After you read it to these people, inquire whether they can think of anything else that you love that you may have forgotten. Ask if they can think of anything that's quintessentially you at your best. In doing so, you ask close, personal intimates to highlight an aspect of your Spirit that you perhaps overlook or don't readily acknowledge.

For example, upon hearing my list, my husband immediately reminded me that I love to solve problems quickly and that I take great joy in doing so. This was indeed a love of my Spirit's that I'd overlooked. And both my daughters, after hearing my list, immediately reminded me that I absolutely love to write, something I totally neglected to include. In fact, writing is a favorite rejuvenating activity, and I completely forgot this about my Spirit.

If you're questioning your path, your truth, and your purpose, begin your exploration with the list you just made. It's the perfect place to find answers and direction because it reflects the authentic you in action.

For example, I just returned from teaching a workshop in San Francisco, where a young woman shared with me that she had no idea what her purpose in life was and felt she was wasting it working as a secretary for a large advertising agency. After I asked her to review what she loved as a way to connect to her purpose, she mentioned that she grew up in Kansas and loved animals. In particular, she loved horses more than anything on Earth. She delighted in riding them, grooming them, competing on them, training them, and anything else that had to do with them. She especially felt that they were healing for her Spirit, and she realized that she missed these animals very much.

As we conversed, she also said that she loved teaching and working with young girls—especially those who came from broken homes—something she'd done when she was in college. She'd even been a "Big Sister" to several young girls over the years, and it had brought her great joy. Continuing to explore, she then remembered that she loved being in nature and had often thought of leaving San Francisco and moving to a more rural area.

By the time she'd finished exploring her loves, she realized that what called her Spirit was working with horses and perhaps finding a way to help adolescent girls build their confidence by learning to ride, which she could teach them to do. She actually decided right then and there that she would move to Lake Tahoe and begin working with horses in the winter. By the time we finished speaking, her Spirit had taken over in full force. The light was in her eyes, the fire burned in her belly, and the clarity to do what she loved took over her mind. I'm not sure if she'll follow through or not, but I do know that she left feeling completely connected to her Spirit, and happier for it!

I spoke with another student in the workshop who had been a scientific researcher for more than 20 years. When asked what she loved, she said, "Children." When I encouraged her to elaborate, she realized that she loved to teach and spend time with kids and often dreamed of creating her own Montessori school. As she spoke, she also came to the conclusion that being a scientific researcher, although something she was good at, wasn't what her Spirit loved at all. Rather, it was something she pursued to please her highly ambitious father. She was extremely bored and uninspired in her present job and dreaded going to work each day. Her Spirit felt isolated and disconnected from all she loved, and she could no longer bear it. Even her father's approval, which her ego felt that it needed, wasn't enough to make her choice worthwhile.

Once she reconnected to her Spirit, she was moved to make a change in the direction it called her to. She left, promising herself that she was going to follow her Spirit and engage in what she really wanted to do. She declared, "I'm going to start my school. The very thought of this makes me happy and inspired. I'm not afraid." When she announced this, the entire class erupted in applause. When one person follows his or her Spirit, it gives us all permission to do the same. As there is only one Spirit, so one person's liberation from fear and ego is everyone else's as well.

The more you give your Spirit what it loves, the stronger and more embodied it becomes; and the more embodied it becomes, the less lost and out of control you feel. A well-nurtured, fully embodied Spirit quiets your nervous, insecure, self-sabotaging, fearful ego mind completely and moves you toward what makes you happy and fills you with light. You stop worrying, and like dominos falling in place, you find yourself on a path toward fulfilling your most authentic self.

The more you know your Spirit and allow it to move you in the direction of what you love, the more quickly you enter into a comfortable and grounded pattern of ease and confidence. You don't have to think about your purpose because you'll be flowing *with* it.

Nurture the desire to know your Spirit. Pay attention to the things that speak to your heart. Follow those clues and you'll travel directly toward what you seek in life . . . always.

You may have temporary relapses of ego and drift away from your Spirit, getting caught up in the traps of negativity and insecurity, but try not to worry about it. Simply engage in one thing your Spirit loves every day and you'll get back on track.

Simple Practice: Dare to Be Happy

Recently I was invited to a barbeque in the back-yard of a good friend. Being unacquainted with most of the other guests present, I listened to the conversations before I joined in. Most of what I heard centered on people's misery or challenges. Not surprisingly, the general theme among the guests was: "I'd be okay if only something or other were different in my life."

There were sympathetic reverberations throughout the crowd as people shared their varying woes, most of which I could very much relate to. There were discussions about the struggles of raising kids (I knew them well), about family members who were physically ill (I have those, too), about rising property taxes (ours have gone through the roof), about challenging partnerships (mine is among the best), and about additional realities of living in the physical, human world with other people.

As I listened, I noticed a tremendous energetic pull to be "simpatico" with those present by chiming in with woes of my own. But I know that it's far more self-loving to be positive and peaceful in spite of all life's problems, and I resisted the temptation to commiserate. Troubles or not, my Spirit prefers to be happy, so I chimed in with positive conversation.

When I shared my peaceful state with the other guests, the discussion came to an uncomfortable halt, and those I was speaking with quickly moved away. I tried a few more

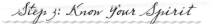

attempts at being generally positive, only to realize that it just wasn't popular to be so cheerful.

What I experienced instead were strained smiles and a few condescending "Lucky you's," followed by a "How come you get to be so special?" Or people simply let the conversation die by acting suddenly distracted and walking away.

I'm not sharing this story to elicit sympathy. I just want to point out that choosing to be happy and filled with self-love won't necessarily win you any popularity contests, especially when there's what other authors call "a currency of misery" in our culture to which most of us are addicted. This currency is the ego running the show. It loves to *share* misery because it only *feels* misery. It doesn't know anything else. So of course people who don't know that they're Spirit, and don't connect with *their* Spirit, fall under the ego's spell and complain. If you don't resonate with other people's egos, those egos get quite annoyed with you as a ploy to intimidate you into being a party to their unhappiness. After all, misery does love company.

So beware of this potential ambush, and stay alert. Don't get intimidated into commiserating on an ego level with others as a way to be connected. Be true to your Spirit, and don't be embarrassed to feel good about yourself. You may initially feel a bit out of sync with the world, and in fact you are: You're out of sync with the dominant energy of the general populace, which is the griping ego at its worst. Stick with loving yourself and living your Spirit, and be patient with others. Although it's hard to believe at times, there *are* people resonating at a higher level of vibration, and if yours is consistently high, you'll connect to them. In the meantime, stay true to your Spirit and enjoy your peace, even if it's unpopular.

Recognize assaults on or judgments of your happiness as attacks from the ego and laugh them off. As you raise your vibration and simply take the higher road, those who are deeply mired in the muck of ego will challenge you. See such challenges as opportunities to show these very same people another way. Their reaction may not be positive at first, but you'll give them something to think about. Have compassion when you're confronted with serial negativity, and see the moment as a chance for you to spread a little joy their way. You never know how it will affect them in the long run, and you may be surprised.

A dear client traveled with her aunt to a small town in Iowa to buy candy made at a local convent by nuns who were famous for their confections. Shortly after loading up on their famed caramels, my client took a bite, savored the flavor, and turned to her aunt with lighthearted exuberance and said, "I really enjoy this caramel. And I'm so grateful that I'm able to savor such sweetness in life."

To which her aunt sharply retorted, "You *should* be grateful, young lady, because goodness knows, you don't deserve such sweetness or anything else God gives you."

Wow! That was enough negativity to knock the sweetness right out of the caramel—and out of my client's heart, too. Fortunately, this assault didn't hit the mark of shame it was headed for. My client did love herself, her Spirit was enjoying the candy tremendously, and she wasn't about to let her aunt's sour grapes take that away from her. She just smiled and took another bite.

They returned home and soon parted ways. My client laughed off the remark and didn't give it another thought. Six months later she received a surprise package in the mail: It was a box of caramels from the monastery, sent by her aunt. In it there was a note that read: "You so enjoyed these caramels that I wanted to send you some more. Just knowing they are sweetening your day sweetens mine."

My client was shocked. Apparently her decision to remain in the vibration of self-love had made a lasting impression on her aunt. From the note, she could tell that her aunt's Spirit had been touched that day and, unbeknownst to her, had awakened. Looking back, she found that this made the trip all the more sweet.

My point is that you not take anyone's resistance to your joy personally. Choosing self-love challenges the collective paradigm of guilt and shame that has controlled us for thousands of years. If we go the route of the ego, we'll never feel worthy of self-love. If we choose to live our Spirit, we'll be instantly liberated. And, moreover, by our example, we'll help others liberate themselves as well . . . not immediately, perhaps, but eventually.

My spiritual teacher taught me this lesson when he said, "The way to help the miserable of the world is not to be one of them." That's simple enough. So although it may be unpopular, it is, nevertheless, loving to others to love yourself and live your Spirit.

It can be lonely to choose self-love. You'll be challenged and, undoubtedly, be tested. Don't take the negative resistance and challenges of others personally. If anything, see them as a sign that you're breaking free from the pernicious vicious cycle of self-loathing and self-controlling ego that's causing so much pain. The greater the opposition you feel and face, the greater the indication that you're succeeding in moving back to the self-love of Spirit.

Judging yourself and others is a soul disease, similar to the flu. Anyone consumed with what I call the "psychic flu" of negativity is quite ill and feels like crap. Have compassion. Have mercy. But have common sense as well. Realize that this kind of energetic flu is contagious and can seize upon even the healthiest among us. Be glad that your self-love gives you resistance. With practice, it will confer complete immunity.

No matter what comes your way, stay true to your commitment to love your Spirit, and don't get pulled off center by others' judgments. Recognize that other people may not be spiritually healthy, and forgive them. God wants you to be happy, joyous, and free—He commands you to be so. Stay true to your Spirit and honor the Creator. Insist on enjoying life no matter what.

STEP 4

Connect with Your Soul Family

Simple Lesson: Connect with Your Soul Family

This step helps you focus on surrounding yourself with your personal soul family—those people who witness and strengthen the authentic you. It emphasizes your Spirit's need to be in community with kindred Spirits and shows you how to find them. The practice that follows helps you set intentions that serve your Spirit every day. As you align with your authentic self, you'll begin to feel deep and genuine love and affection for who you really are.

Connecting with family is one of the most deeply restorative acts of self-love we can choose. Our Spirit regenerates best when in the company of kindred Spirits, and to be cut off from this resource is debilitating to it. We're pack animals by nature; and we need our tribe— our people—to help lift our Spirit, strengthen our energy fields, and reflect our authentic selves back to us.

This ideally occurs with family-of-origin members. But "family" for Spirit doesn't necessarily mean blood relations. Just as we have a "bloodline" made up of those who share our genetic makeup, so do we also have a "soul line." Yours is composed of kindred Spirits who energetically see, know, and resonate with you on a deep and authentic level without dialogue, explanation, or effort. They just "get" you, as you do them.

The important thing about connecting with family, when it comes to loving and living your Spirit, is that healthy kinship bonds remind you to be true to your Spirit and bring you back to yourself better than you can do alone.

Whenever I'm with *my* family, for example, especially my siblings, it's only a matter of minutes before I find myself relaxing, laughing, and remembering my authentic self. Any self-doubts or anxious thoughts I'm carrying begin to quiet. My humor kicks in, and I suddenly feel that I'm once again "home."

When I'm with my family, I feel seen, witnessed, understood, and comfortable in my own skin. I forget about my outer self, my ego self, my "story," or my external identity. I stop being "someone," and I just *am*.

This isn't to suggest that my family doesn't have our struggles, fights, issues, complaints, and irritations. We're a bunch of hotheaded French Romanians, so we have plenty of differences to banter about. But those disputes exist only on the ego level. Even with them in place, we nevertheless rejuvenate each other on a soul level. Something energetically positive occurs when we're together, and we feel better.

I've noticed that the same occurs for my husband when he's with *his* family. Nothing quite regenerates

Patrick's Spirit more than several hours with his brothers and sisters, in spite of the fact that he's the eldest child in a large Catholic family, with all of its predictable pathologies fully in place. Something deep within him lights up, calms down, gets reconnected, and satisfies his soul. All the time in the world with me doesn't do for him energetically what his brothers and sisters do. It's not that they're better . . . they're just different.

The benefit of being with family isn't intellectual or even emotional—it's energetic. In Patrick's case, he has had huge intellectual and emotional differences with all of his siblings at one time or another, as have they with him. It doesn't matter. The benefit he feels when around them is strictly vibrational. His Spirit is affirmed in their company, and it makes him happy.

I believe that we all have soul connections with at least some family-of-origin members who affirm our Spirit and help prevent us from getting totally lost in the confusion and drain of ego identity. Whether it's a sibling, parent, cousin, or grandparent, there's always at least one member of your family constellation who does see you, the Divine authentic you, and can perceive you correctly. This relative is the one who reminds you to believe in yourself and to know that you're loved as *you*. He or she is there to keep you from becoming totally lost or disconnected from your Spirit.

Drawing support from bloodline family members may feel impossible to some people. I hear many lament that their family doesn't "get" them, and they withdraw in anger and grief. If this is the case for you, it's important to assess honestly whether you've given your family a fair chance to "get you" by revealing yourself openly before you cut them off.

Just today I was on separate conference calls with a mother and son, both frustrated and deeply injured by their experience of not being witnessed lovingly by the other. The mother was a woman who devoted her life to her son, financing his education, apartment, car, auto insurance, and wardrobe; and as a result of spending this money, she felt angry that her son treated her with such disrespect.

"He doesn't appreciate me," she lamented, and hers wasn't an ego complaint, but rather a heartfelt Spirit wound.

He, on the other hand, maintained her lawn; took care of her animals; and painted her house, including beautiful murals on the walls of her living room. "She doesn't appreciate me," he complained.

While both showed up quite dutifully in each other's lives, the problem was that this was the *only* way they showed up for each other. They didn't talk—they didn't know what the other loved, cared about, believed in, or dreamed of. In other words, they didn't know each other's Spirit. They only experienced the other's disappointments.

The mother, for example, was an extraordinary money manager and, unbeknownst to her son, had created and administered a fund that fed and housed more than 20 homeless women annually, providing medical care and job training for them as well. She was a deeply compassionate humanitarian, yet he had no idea. This part of her expressed her most authentic Spirit; however, her son only knew her to be a bossy mom who only cared about money, because this was all she revealed to him.

Meanwhile, he wrote beautiful songs and composed wonderful music, some of which he performed in various local amateur plays. He was incrementally adding to the beauty of the world, yet his mother had no idea he possessed these musical talents. Why would she? He'd never revealed this facet of himself—his true, authentic self— to her. She only saw him as a "dreamer" who didn't work a regular, or in her perception, "real," job.

By hiding their true selves from one another, they robbed themselves and each other of the deeper connection their souls were capable of enjoying. They settled for a less-than-authentic connection of ego to ego, rather than risk the discomfort of revealing their Spirits to one another.

I find that people make this mistake, especially in families, all the time. The potential for a profound soul connection is there, but it's up to the Spirit within each person to see it, want it, and create it. When we relate to one another ego to ego, we can't see these deeper connections at all. The ego views everyone as a potential enemy, even family members. When we relate to one another Spirit to Spirit, we see and feel our Divine connection right away.

My role in consulting with both mother and son on the same day was orchestrated by their Spirits to help them see each other more accurately and to reestablish a genuine soul connection once again.

After they learned of one another's generous and creative Spirit in action, their perceptions opened up. I suggested that the mother attend one of her son's concerts. I also recommended that the son go with her to the shelter she sponsored and observe how she helped the women there by teaching them new skills. They agreed that this was a good idea, and said that they would.

Several weeks later I received a note explaining how, after they got better acquainted, they developed a new-found respect for one another. They started talking and decided to combine talents. He and his friends would put on a concert to raise money for the homeless women, and she would approach her business associates to help sponsor it. No longer unaware of each other's most beautiful qualities, they became friends and allies. I'm certain that this was their soul plan all along.

I share this story to suggest that before you decide that your family of origin has no capacity to witness you accurately, ask yourself if you've given them a fair opportunity to do so. And "fair" means going through the muck of uncovering a genuine connection.

For example, I have a dear friend who was born into an extremely toxic, alcoholic family rooted in strong Southern Baptist beliefs that judged a great deal of the human race to be less than morally acceptable. Being gay, he originally decided that his family was much too morally righteous and conservative to ever accept his sexual orientation, and he withdrew from their influence altogether by moving to another city. Not wanting to hide his true nature, he didn't conceal his sexuality from his family, but neither did he afford them the chance to assimilate this information in his presence. He simply assumed that they would reject him, so he sent them what amounted to a good-bye letter just before he left.

Not surprisingly, at first he didn't receive a response. In fact, several years went by without any communication from his family at all. Then, out of the blue, his sister—who was ten years younger than he was—showed up unannounced on his doorstep. Shocked, he invited her in and asked her, quite defensively, what she was doing there. After several hours of sobbing . . . and raging, challenging, and confronting him . . . she made it crystal clear that, although his parents weren't energetically equipped to be part of his true spiritual family, she was. And he'd never given her that chance. He'd cut her off from him even though she needed him as part of her soul family.

The wounds weren't forgotten overnight, but an energetic healing did occur on the spot. The minute they reconnected on a Spirit level, they both recovered a significant energy loss that his sudden leaving had caused them. Theirs was a difficult relationship, but worth it. Through their struggles, they helped each other become more authentic and connect to their Spirit in a way that no other person could have.

His parents never did connect with him once he left, and both died young, but he and his sister stayed connected and continue to enjoy self-love and self-celebration on the deepest level.

❀

That said, it's still nevertheless true that relatives may at times not provide the soul food your Spirit needs to feel deeply loved. If, after exploring all possibilities for true connection, you feel on a soul level that nobody who can witness your Spirit is in your bloodline, then it's time to explore your *soul lines:* those souls embodied in current time with you who have been part of your bloodline in past lives and *do* know, witness, and love you unconditionally.

You recognize members of your soul line instantly because you like them so much, want them to be in your life, and feel completely at ease with them immediately. Although you may not intellectually know why you sense such a strong connection, you feel authentic and at peace in their presence. Their vibration energizes your Spirit.

When you're with a soul-family member, your conscious focus may be spiritual, or it may not be. For example, you might meet a neighbor and find that you both absolutely love to cook, and suddenly the two of you have tremendous fun when you get together in the kitchen. You may never speak about the soul or Spirit in any way. You may only talk about sugar and flour. But your souls are fed when you're together. And in that way, it's all spiritual.

When it comes to being with a soul-family member, what's obvious is that in the presence of this person, you feel instantly better, stronger, happier, and more alive than before. Your body is relaxed. Your thoughts lighten up. Your fears vanish. You don't focus on the past or the future. You're simply present . . . and, most of all, you feel good about yourself—in fact, you *love* yourself.

Some members of my soul family share my line of work, but others don't. I have an entire group of soul-family members in France who don't even fully know, or care, what I do. They just like who I am, and vice versa. They energize me on an entirely different level from that of my spiritual-teacher self. They energize and witness my traveling, adventurous, shopping, and artistic self. Every time I'm with them, I feel as though I'm receiving the energetic equivalent of a blood transfusion—I'm positively renewed. I need my connection to them. They feed my Spirit and bring joy to my life. They also help me experience deep joy in being *me*.

Such soul connections are essential components of loving yourself. Recognize these relationships and value them. Do whatever it takes to commune with your soul-family members regularly. Fortunately, you have them everywhere you go. They can be found by simply following your heart.

Simple Practice: Lead with Your Spirit

When you wake up in the morning, start your day with gratitude. No matter how you feel or what's going on in your life, pay attention to the fact that merely being alive for another day is a gift from your Creator. Quietly or out loud—whatever you prefer—acknowledge what you're grateful for. It can be as simple as: "I am grateful that I woke up this morning," "I am grateful that I am able to think," or "I am grateful that I am breathing."

Start by acknowledging three things for which you're grateful. As you train yourself to focus on your blessings every morning, the list will grow. You need only take a few moments for this exercise. It isn't necessary to recite everything you're thankful for. Just notice a few things and then genuinely express gratitude for them.

Being grateful is a highly self-loving choice. It shifts your attention away from the things that upset, frighten, annoy, frustrate, or depress you; and it infuses your body with positive, healing vibrations. Gratitude also rejuvenates your cells, slows your heart rate, and relaxes your muscles. It's a nice thing to do for *you*. It feels good.

After you express gratitude, next check in with your Spirit and ask it to lead you this day. To do so, stand up, place both feet on the floor, take a deep breath in through the nose, and then exhale out through the mouth, releasing the sound "Ahh." Breathing in this way opens your heart and invites your Spirit to enter your body more fully.

If you notice stress, tension, or worry, continue breathing as suggested until you feel centered, grounded, and relaxed. Each time you inhale, mentally welcome your Divine Spirit into your body, remembering that you're inviting your most sacred, beloved self to lead. Feel the presence of your Spirit as it centers fully in your body. Notice how the energy of your Spirit fills your lungs, your heart, your mind, and finally your cells with light. Enjoy this feeling. Next, envision your Spirit fully descending into your body, settling comfortably in your bones and making itself at home.

Don't rush this exercise. Take your time. The ego likes to race "headfirst" into the day, creating a false sense of urgency or emergency . . . while the Spirit enters the body "heart-first": slowly, peacefully, calmly.

Once you feel grounded and centered in your Spirit, place both hands over your solar plexus (which basically means just above your belly button). This is your third chakra, better known as your power center. This is the energetic point in your body from which you make decisions and direct your life. It's also the place from which your Spirit moves into the world.

Imagine your Spirit's presence expanding from your heart to your belly, fully encompassing both. Do this by continuing to breathe comfortably while envisioning your body filling up with a bright light.

Next, with both hands on your belly, imagine standing in your power, and say out loud, "The most important thing for my Spirit to focus on today is _____," and then fill in the blank. For example, you might say, "The most important thing for my Spirit to focus on today is writing in my journal," "The most important thing for my Spirit to focus on today is spending time with my partner," or "The most important thing for my Spirit to focus on today is going to the gym."

Be patient and allow your Spirit to reveal the answer rather than having your brain come up with a response. Focus on one Spirit intention or goal for that day. The ego mind loves to make long to-do lists. This sets up the pressure of obligations and duties and leaves you wide open to failure, because no matter how good your intentions, life comes in waves of energy. It bends and flows . . . and throws in all kinds of surprises as well.

So if you have long to-do lists to attend to, you have a very high probability of getting derailed. You'll feel defeated. Furthermore, you also have a great chance of missing synchronistic opportunities if your mind overloads you with obligations. The Spirit prefers to keep life simple. You need only name one important priority for the day and attend to that in order for your Spirit to be happy. So start by identifying the goal most important to your Spirit, and then relax as you move toward it. If your Spirit absolutely must name more than one intention, cite the others—but not as goals, only as "preferences."

For example, on a recent morning my Spirit's number one goal was to spend some quality time with my entire family over dinner. My preference was that we have a home-cooked meal, but being together was the most important goal and the one I committed my Spirit to. I knew that no matter what unfolded that day, if I had dinner with my family, at the end of it my Spirit would be happy.

This was an important Spirit goal because my daughters are now 18 and 19 and are going in directions of their own. I rarely see them. Also, my husband takes French and painting classes at night, so he's frequently out as well. I often teach in the evenings or am traveling, so family dinners are fewer and farther between. Family time isn't easy to arrange, and our respective interests compete with our together time with a vengeance.

Once my Spirit's intention was set, I began the day by asking everyone to be home for dinner by 6 P.M. At first the girls hemmed and hawed, citing other plans, but I said that it was important to my Spirit, and I'd greatly appreciate their company, if only for a quick meal. So knowing that it was important to me, everyone agreed. Then we all went our separate ways.

At 5:15 P.M., the skies suddenly darkened and before I could fully register what was happening, a tornado watch was sounded for our area—for the first time I can remember as long as I've lived in Chicago.

Fighting panic, I picked up the phone to track everyone down and make certain they were safe and knew of the danger. Feeling the unexpected threat, with rain pounding on the house as I dialed, I realized beyond a doubt just how important to my Spirit being with my family was that day. In fact, nothing on Earth was more crucial at that moment.

Within minutes of the alarm, the phone rang three separate times: First there was Sabrina, saying she was safe and nearby; second was Patrick, also safe and nearby; and finally, to my relief, my elusive older daughter, Sonia, also called to say she was safe and nearby.

Within 20 minutes, we were all huddled together in the kitchen, the violent storm passing overhead. As we breathed a collective sigh of relief, I couldn't help but thank and love my Spirit for having requested together time that morning. Because I'd done that, everyone had stayed closer to home than they normally would have, and consequently we were able to quickly regroup while under a threat.

Such is the beauty of honoring the Spirit: It knows what the ego can't. Had I not loved my Spirit enough to listen to its priority and request that we have dinner together, who knows where everyone might have been when all hell broke loose? Thank God I didn't have to find out. My loving Spirit spared us all the unnecessary anxiety and drama of being separated.

The city of Chicago suffered the loss of hundreds of trees that day, but miraculously no loss of life. In spite of the worst weather event in the city's history, it was the best dinner I'd ever had with my family. We were together and safe, and there was nothing better I could have asked for.

Honoring your Spirit and giving it priority not only is the most self-loving way to live your life, it's also the most loving thing you can do for others. By identifying your Spirit's top priority each day and making it your goal, you assure not only the highest expression of your own self, but you also ensure that you bring the highest, most authentic vibration of *you* to others. This sets up a cascade effect of positive energy for all to feel and invites enormous synchronicity into your life and relationships as well.

End the day the way you began it: with gratitude. No matter what goal or intention you started out with, at the close of the day acknowledge just how perfectly it did in fact unfold, and be grateful for the gifts it brought you. By doing so, you affirm that you trust your authentic Spirit, and not your ego, to lead. Whatever did take place, it happened because your Spirit wanted to have that experience. Events may not go as you—or your ego—consciously wished or planned, but they always occur as your Spirit requires in accordance with the Divine plan. Accepting this is a huge step toward loving yourself.

Take a few grounding breaths again—in through the nose and out through the mouth—and enjoy how good this feels. Notice how extremely self-loving it is to breathe in so deeply and become quietly centered.

Next, review your day with an eye toward the gifts it brought. What transpired that your Spirit loved most? What blessing showed up unexpectedly? What are you grateful for?

You can review your day silently or write down your daily gifts in a journal. Better yet, if possible, share these gifts with someone you love who will listen to your Spirit with appreciation.

Right before I go to bed, I share the gifts I received that day with my husband and encourage him to do the same with me.

The night of the storm, as I looked out the window, seeing 100-year-old trees downed across the city, I was thankful for the catalpa tree still standing proudly in front of our house. As I noticed lights out in homes, damaged fences, and flooding everywhere, I was grateful and amazed that our old Victorian was still standing, intact and dry. As I imagined neighbors calling to check on family members in the outlying areas, only to get busy signals because power lines were down, I was thrilled to have been able to sit with all members of *my* family beside me. It had been a good day.

When you end your day with gratitude, you end it with power. That's because no matter what your ego's intentions, or the results, it's never satisfied—it always wants more. But what your Spirit desires is always *more* than enough . . . it's perfect peace.

STEP 5

Keep the Balance

Simple Lesson: Keep the Balance

This step sensitizes you to the energetic costs of living in an ego-based world and guides you to replenish your Spirit when drained and overtaxed. The practice that follows will further connect you to your Creative Source, which will protect you from the negativity that abounds in such an ego-based world. Through meditation, you'll tap into the endless store of love and devotion the Universe has for you.

❋

One of the most important and overlooked aspects of self-love, and one that I believe we all could do well to become more mindful of, is the energetic toll that day-to-day life exacts upon us. We need to properly assess our psychic expenditures so that we can replenish ourselves properly as we go along. Otherwise, we unwittingly fall into energetic depletions that leave us vulnerable to negativity and fatigue.

Let's face it—other people, events, and even things all require some amount of energy from us. Fortunately, they replenish that energy as well. Our assignment as consciously self-loving, Divine spiritual beings is to accurately measure these energetic expenditures so that we can keep our balance. Given the demands of day-to-day life, we must replenish ourselves frequently with self-loving choices and actions to keep our Spirit light-hearted and energized.

For example, presently one of my top priorities is traveling and sharing tools for higher awareness and intuitive awakening around the world. I do this mostly through leading workshops and having private consul-tations. I really love my work—the travel, teaching, and people; as well as sharing with others the tools I possess for Spirited living.

Yet, even though all this is true, at the same time my work is energetically taxing on me. The travel, the classes, and talking with people cause energetic wear and tear . . . not to mention the stress of frequently sleeping in noisy hotels, constantly eating restaurant food, and being disoriented in new territory. At the end of a trip or workshop, I feel both exhilarated and energetically spent at the same time.

To counterbalance these situations, when I travel I bring plenty of resources to replenish me along the way. These include my iPod, noise-reducing headphones, my own pillow and blanket, a bottle of Rescue Remedy, small scented candles, chocolate, my computer, and a good novel.

These rejuvenating necessities renew my Spirit, and I use them to help me stay in balance. Just knowing that I have these things available to comfort my Spirit at the

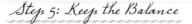

end of the day keeps me grounded and peaceful. When traveling, I also do one more thing: I refrain from socializing. I stay inside, remain quiet, and rest. This gives my Spirit the peace it needs to restore itself.

This energetic "overdraft" isn't something that only I am aware of. In fact, I've spoken to hundreds of people about this very subject. It's very common for students to write or call me after a class and tell me what a high they got from the experience, only to return home and crash into a slump 48 to 72 hours later. This doesn't happen because someone missed the point of the workshop. Rather, it happens because, although positive, the experience of learning something new (especially in *my* classroom) can be energetically demanding and requires such heightened attention that a person's basic vitality can get tapped.

Everyday life—especially those situations that require change, even when it's positive—can deplete and tax us energetically, so we must be mindful of ways to replenish our energy if we are to be truly self-loving.

One of the best and most natural ways to rebalance and refresh our vitality and spring back after an energetic expenditure is to rest. When I give or attend a workshop, I try to take a mini-nap or a quick meditative break at lunch if at all possible. It greatly restores my energy and revives my Spirit. It's very self-loving and helps keep me in balance.

We can also revive by doing something fun, like watching a movie, calling a good friend and chatting for a few minutes, taking an Epsom-salt bath, or going to a wonderful restaurant where the waitstaff are attentive and the food is full of flavor and spice. There are countless ways in which to reenergize and love the Spirit.

Being sensitive to the toll that life takes on you and lovingly allowing yourself to adjust to and balance these demands is a vital act of self-love. When you don't register the energetic cost of your daily life, you fail to rebalance and refuel your Spirit, which leads to resentment, depression, and exhaustion. In fact, I believe that neglecting to renew the Spirit is one of the biggest culprits in the epidemics of chronic fatigue, fibromyalgia, and Epstein-Barr syndrome. Quite simply, the Spirit is overtaxed and isn't given adequate time to renew. This is especially true in Western society, where we're pushed to go beyond our limits every single day.

We don't need a crisis to justify a break. Everyday interactions, especially when emotionally volatile, can be highly depleting to the Spirit. For example, I have a dear friend who's caring for her two elderly parents. She's very close to both of them and makes a point of spending time with them at least twice a week, just to check in and stay involved in their lives. In addition, because they're still independent but slowing down considerably, she also buys their groceries, runs errands for them, oversees their finances, and tries to get them out of the house for exercise and recreation. She loves that she's able to do all of this for them and is grateful that they're still in fairly good health. Yet, because they're seniors, they're set in their ways and prone to becoming cranky and inflexible, both with her and each other. So being with them is a challenge.

Although my friend treasures her time with her parents, when she comes home, she feels tired, depleted, and "wiped out." This isn't because she doesn't want to be with her mom and dad or help them. Rather, when visiting them, my friend does everything in her power to be aware, patient, nonjudgmental, and loving no matter what her parents say or do—and this takes energy.

Before she realized just how demanding to her Spirit these interactions were, she'd return home from her outings only to find that in a relatively short time she was overly reactive, critical, cross, or impatient with her husband and sons. Feeling ashamed and embarrassed about her behavior, she realized that all the good vibes she'd hoped to create went out the window. She began to attack her Spirit with self-judgment and criticism in every way.

We spoke about these frequent energetic flare-ups recently, and I pointed out that she wasn't giving herself the time to renew her Spirit between visits, and this was why she was so reactive when she returned home. Her Spirit was running on empty after she came back from spending time with her parents, and she just needed a little rest and rejuvenation and some TLC to bring it back into balance. If she allowed for that, chances were much greater that she wouldn't snap at her family and fall into a vicious cycle of guilt and depletion.

I reminded her that while it was wonderful to be with her parents, doing so took work, and I suggested that she allow herself some alone time to regenerate after each visit. I also proposed that she ask for nurturing from other family members, perhaps in the form of a foot rub or a few minutes undisturbed for a bubble bath when she returned home, to help her refuel her Spirit. At first she thought that these suggestions were excessive and self-indulgent, as the ego so often does. She felt them to be a little "touchy-feely" for her self-image and rejected the idea on the spot. Yet after repeated arguments and petty clashes following her parental outings, she rethought the suggestion and gave it a try.

She became more sensitive to her Spirit; asked her family to go out to dinner on the nights she was with her mother and father; and came home to a quiet house, a warm bubble bath, and an early bedtime. With these choices, the drain and conflicts ended.

Attending to her parents started to be the loving experience she desired, and her family enjoyed being supportive by giving her a little space to be alone afterward. She discovered the power of rest and rejuvenation and no longer felt guilty about it. The results were simply too positive to deny. Her Spirit was grateful, and her life improved all around.

The key to keeping your Spirit in balance is to recognize the need for rest and rejuvenation every day and not to approach it with an "if necessary" attitude. Rather, plan your energetic recuperation in advance as part of a self-loving way of life, and look forward to your quiet time. It's good for your Spirit, and it's good for others', too. As you love and live your Spirit, others will see that it's important as well.

The other night my daughter came home from her fourth highly successful (according to her), very hot date in only four nights with a new guy, only to accidentally touch her bare calf to the tailpipe of his motorcycle as she was getting off of it. (Yes, she was on a motorcycle; and no, I didn't approve—but that's another story.)

She received a fairly bad burn on her leg and had to go to a lot of trouble to care for it and prevent it from becoming infected. Not surprisingly from an energetic perspective, this mishap created a pause in her dating tempo with the guy. Her burn also resulted in a lot of love and fussing over her on the part of her doting, protective family (us) and gave her a solid excuse to slow future dates with this guy to a more manageable pace.

The not-so-minor burn counterbalanced the "hot date" and helped her re-center herself. Of course, all of this was on an unconscious level and not planned . . . yet the Spirit does find ways to take care of itself. I'm not suggesting that burning her leg was an intentional act of self-love. But underneath the "accident," I'm sure that there was a need for her Spirit to recuperate the vast amounts of energy she'd expended on this new guy in a short time, and the incident provided a convenient way to do that. Although painful, her burn did inadvertently help rebalance her energy and bring her back to self. She slowed down, they switched from dates on his motor-cycle to ones in a borrowed car, and the slower pace was clearly more comfortable for my daughter, as I could tell by her behavior.

I know that this may seem like a stretch to people not accustomed to examining life on an energetic level, as I do, but if you stop and objectively look over your own life experiences, I'm certain that you, too, will notice your own Spirit's unconscious attempts to rebal-ance your energy when you're overextended. It can show up in something as coincidental as getting a cold and becoming bedridden after helping your best friend move all weekend; hurting your back after working a 100-hour workweek; or, as I've been known to do, going on a shopping spree that's hard to control after a particu-larly rigorous schedule of workshops.

My point is, the soul *does* try to refresh your Spirit's energy for you in some way. Rather than reach a crisis point that requires dramatic intervention on your Spir-it's part, it's so much more self-aware and self-loving of you to give yourself full freedom and permission to recu-perate consciously—and plan to do so in advance. Then your recovery is pain free, and self-love remains intact.

Simple Practice: Meditate

If you were in the middle of a very hot, dry desert and became extremely thirsty, would you hesitate to stop and drink if you were near an oasis? Of course not— in fact, you probably would want to stay near that oasis and have water every day. I know *I* would.

Well, that's what meditating is like for the Spirit: It's a cool, refreshing drink at the wellspring of life, available to anyone, anywhere, anytime they're willing to take their attention off of the scorching intensity of being part of the human ego condition.

Meditation is refreshment, replenishment, and rejuvenation for the Spirit—and it's a vacation for the ego and body as well. When you meditate, your Spirit checks in with God, your Creator, Who is the source for the fulfillment of all your needs.

The beauty of meditation is that there's no one right way to do it; there's simply *your* way. The ego mind discourages you from meditating by having you believe that it's a near-impossible yogi-like feat that's only legitimate if you can silence your brain to the point of becoming nearly unconscious.

How appealing is that? Not very, which is why this is such an effective ploy to keep you from trying it. Your Spirit knows better. Meditation is simply a walk with God. You enter it through your imagination, and once there, you can accompany the Divine anywhere you want. You can walk with God along a pristine sandy beach at sunrise; through a green, earthy forest and into a magical glen; to a gorgeous mountain peak overlooking an ancient valley; or to a distant star. Or you can simply invite God to join you in a fireside chat in your den if you aren't up for wandering too far.

As you walk with God, imagine that you're talking with Him. Tell your Creator all that troubles your heart. Unload everything, as God knows all anyway, so there's no need to hold back or hide. Take your time as you unburden yourself. Breathe gently in and out as you share your concerns, enjoying the walk as you confess your troubles. Then, after you've emptied your heart and there are no more words for the moment, continue the walk with God in silence. Or, if you're enjoying a fireside chat, once you're through revealing your burdens, just watch the fire with God. Enjoy the silence and the scenery. Relish being close and connected to God. As you walk, imagine that your Creator is lovingly embracing you. Imagine being hugged by God.

It's possible that God may break the silence and advise you while on your meditative walk, but then again, He may simply love you instead. Be okay with whatever unfolds. Just enjoy being in God's loving vibration and healing presence.

Walk as long as you want, and when your Spirit is full of God's presence, return with God to the door of your imagination. Thank your Creator for His presence and love, and step back through the door and into the present time.

That's it. You've meditated. See, it's simple.

Some days you'll walk longer with God than others. Just be certain to go for a walk or meet with God every day, because it restores and energizes your Spirit. If you go to the door of your imagination to meditate regularly, especially at a specific time, God will know when you're coming to see Him and will be waiting to welcome you with an open, loving embrace the moment you cross the threshold.

Treasure your time in God's presence. Protect it and don't allow your ego to distract you or steal away this time by making excuses; overbooking your schedule; letting the outside world come first; or getting sidetracked by TV, the phone, or your computer. It would be as debilitating to lose time with God as it would be to allow a scoundrel to lead you away from the oasis back to the dry desert with no sustenance.

If you're still uncertain about meditation and worry about your success, quiet your ego by easing into it. Go for a short imaginary walk with God around your own block or neighborhood. You can venture further in God's company as you become more comfortable. Just remember to keep it simple. The point is to connect with your source . . . to drink at the oasis of Divine love in a dry desert of ego concerns.

INTERLUDE

The Heart
of the Matter

***

The Heart of the Matter

Here, at the heart of the book, we're taking a break from the lessons and practice of self-love and authentic Spirited living, and focusing on how to fully engage the heart. Love is broken down into four basic expressions of true Spirit, corresponding to the four chambers of the heart: the <u>open heart,</u> the <u>clear heart,</u> the <u>wise heart,</u> and the <u>courageous heart.</u> In this section, you'll learn how you can remove any obstacles to experiencing the deepest level of love for your Divine Spirit and thereby gain inner peace.

Have an Open Heart

To love yourself and live your Spirit, you must have a heart that's open. When you do, you're receptive to the love and goodness of God and life. You see, feel, and attract the positive in the world. You connect with the Spirit of life rather than its drama.

You can't experience love of any sort, of self or otherwise, if your heart isn't open—for it's only the open heart that allows you to receive, feel, and experience love of God, life, and others. As a Divine Being, you—and everyone else—are born with the open heart of the sweet, undefended child. It's the heart that expects life to be a positive, wonderful experience.

The open heart looks forward to life. It delights in experience and enjoys the wonders and gifts of being alive. This heart smells the flowers of life, drinks its milk shakes, and plays on its playground. The open heart sees, feels, and absorbs the beauty of the world.

If your heart is closed, you cut yourself off from all the goodness of life. In this state, you won't be able to connect with your Spirit, nor will you be able to enjoy beauty or music or laughter or love. If your heart is closed, you can't feel or experience any of the sweetness that life offers, and you become isolated in your ego.

A friend of mine described having a closed heart as being like a window-shopper looking at the fantastic beauty of life through plate glass: You may be able to see it, but you can't touch it or experience it for yourself. You're locked out.

As I said, we all start out in life with an open heart and a direct connection to our Source, the Holy Divine Mother/Father God. Sadly, we soon begin to experience human ego confusion—such as anger, judgment, and disapproval—which makes us disconnect from our Spirit and close our hearts. This results in pain, disappointment, and injury . . . which in turn causes our egos to panic, closing our hearts even more. We become caught in a vicious cycle of misery.

Through the eyes of the ego, there will always be a million and one reasons for closing your heart. Yet the minute you do so, you disconnect from your Source, which is Divine love. To close your heart for whatever reason is like plucking a flower from the garden and putting it in a drawer. No matter how your ego justifies this act, you deny yourself all love and nurturing from God, life, and others, which you need to grow. Essentially you sentence your Spirit to a slow death.

That's why keeping your heart open is among the most important—and perhaps most challenging—of all decisions you can make to love yourself and live your Spirit. You must maintain an open heart in order to stay in a close and receptive relationship with all that nurtures and supports your Spirit, no matter what disappointments come. Only an open heart assures that life's gifts will keep flowing toward you. Only an open heart sustains your soul in every way.

To maintain this state of being, you only have to make one simple decision: Expect good things. When you do, you claim your right, as a Divine and beloved child of God, to be beautifully provided for and nourished throughout life no matter what unfolds. When you expect good things, you *attract* them. This is the natural Divine plan.

My brother Anthony has had his fair share of challenges in life, some very painful, yet he remains openhearted and always expects good things to come his way.

One day around lunchtime as he was sitting on his front porch with his girlfriend, she turned to him and said, "I'm hungry," and suggested that they get a hamburger from the local burger joint. Not at all interested in her suggestion, he declined, saying, "I'm not in the mood for another burger. I'm in the mood for something delicious, with real flavor and spice."

He had no more gotten the words out of his mouth when they both noticed a young man dressed in a chef's coat and hat walking toward them carrying a covered platter in his hands. Smiling, my brother asked, "What have you got there?"

The young man returned his smile, and explained that he was a student at the local culinary school that had just opened a block away. The platter he carried was a new dish he'd just invented that day. My ever-curious (and perpetually hungry) brother then asked, "What is it?"

"It's shrimp with saffron over rice. It's very spicy and full of flavor," replied the young man.

Not missing a beat, my brother inquired, "Can we try it?"

"Sure," answered the young man, surprised, but obviously pleased by their interest. He then walked directly up to them and handed the platter over, asking, "Do you mind if I stick around to see if you like it?"

"Of course not," they replied, laughing. "Come on in."

The man then proceeded to follow them into their kitchen and presented the meal as if they were seated in a fine restaurant. Not only was the food delicious, but it was served in style. My brother laughed as he told me the story, thrilled at his good fortune and the delightful synchronicity of the Universe. I couldn't help but think, however, that he had received such a remarkable treat because his heart was open enough to say hello and ask the young man what he was carrying.

That's how it works. If your heart is open and you expect the best, the Universe meets you halfway and fills your life with wonderful surprises, as it did for my brother and his girlfriend that day.

Even during the darkest night of the soul, the most self-loving and self-healing choice you can make is to keep your heart open and expect something good to come from your difficulties.

I had a client years ago who was a troubled and unruly teenager, heavily involved in drugs. At age 17, she lost her entire family to a fire and suddenly found herself alone, homeless, and emotionally devastated beyond belief. Although it took quite a while for her to regain her emotional bearings, she eventually realized that she had a choice: Either she could continue to wallow in self-pity and pain and spiral further downward, or she could honor everything her family had ever taught her before they died and use her experience of adversity to grow as a person. Although she would never wish such a terrible loss on anyone, in the most painful way it helped her become stronger.

With her realization, she went from being a self-centered, unfocused, drug-using teenager to a serious, dedicated, hardworking student with a mission. She quit all drugs, got a job, and studied and worked seven days a week. She found purpose and decided that she would indeed honor all she had received from her family by doing something worthwhile in life. She eventually graduated from high school, went directly to college, kept her job, and devoted her free time to working at the student-counseling center, helping fellow young people through losses and challenges. Whereas before the fire her heart had been closed and she cared for nothing besides her own adolescent indulgences, now she opened her heart and was galvanized toward the goal of helping others who were suffering. It took a long time, and it's fair to say that she still has her bad days.

When I last spoke with her, I asked her how she'd managed to get through such a devastating loss. Her answer was simple: "I had to believe that something good would come from my loss and keep my heart open to it. Otherwise, I would have wasted away in grief. Being useful to others is good for me. I now value life and don't intend to ever waste it again."

❀

It's a challenge to keep your heart open when the world hurts you, but to close it at these times is far more painful than anything life throws at you. To do so is to cut yourself off from living. It's spiritual death and self-destruction, and the most painful of all choices you could ever make.

My client Robyn closed her heart at an early age and suffered lifelong consequences. She was the fourth child in a family of seven, and when she was 14, her mother was diagnosed with breast cancer and died 11 months later. Her father was so overwhelmed by her mother's death and the needs of the family that he turned to alcohol and became despondent and violent, which devastated Robyn.

At 16, completely demoralized, she moved out of the house, quit school, and began working as a waitress at the local diner. Robyn decided, following her mother's death and her father's terrible decline, that she would never allow anyone to hurt her again. She closed her heart and tuned the world out. Although she worked hard and was appreciated at her job, she had no friends and few other outlets for affection, save her dog, a German shepherd named Foxy.

Her siblings periodically tried to contact her, but she pushed them away. By the time she was 25, they'd all but given up on her and had moved on. Robyn became increasingly lonely and angry but refused to open her heart and take the chance to let in love of any sort.

When we met, she was 34. She came to me because she'd heard about my work in a radio interview and wanted to know if her life would ever get better. When she arrived, she was defensive and suspicious—and, underneath it all, extremely hurt by life. I explained that her heart was closed due to her earlier trauma, but that unless she opened it once again, she'd remain cut off from life and all the good things it had to offer.

Although she acknowledged that she'd closed her heart, there was no way she was going to take the chance of ever opening it again. Even though she was lonely and wanted to feel better, she wasn't willing to assume the risk of being hurt or disappointed once more. I told her that love was trying to find her, and she admitted that there was a young man she worked with who'd tried several times to ask her out, but she refused to go. I encouraged her to rethink that decision, and she said she would consider it.

Robyn did end up going out with him, and they embarked on a relationship. He fell in love with her and asked her to marry him, but afraid she'd get hurt, she refused. It was too risky to open up that deeply to him. He tried to change her mind over a period of two years, but to no avail. She wouldn't get past her closed heart. Eventually he gave up and left her for another woman. The last time I saw her, she was angrier and more hurt than ever and said that she'd known he couldn't be trusted.

I felt sad for her. Her closed heart had driven away an opportunity to experience love. I didn't see Robyn after that, and I wonder about her sometimes. I wish that I could say I knew she would be all right. I do pray that something might reopen her heart one day. Without an open heart, there's no way life can really improve. With one, it *always* improves.

Basically, the open heart is that of the Divine Child—the heart of your Spirit—and it trusts that the Universe loves you and will provide for you, care for you, protect you, and nurture you as you grow. This heart relaxes and enjoys life.

The open heart is a portal to Heaven and the gateway for your Spirit to enter your body. It's the most powerful center you have. So to love yourself and live your Spirit, always keep your heart open to the Universe's gifts. Expect good things from life even when its challenges are overwhelming. God has a plan, and positive things are always in store for you, but remember that you can only receive them if your heart is open.

I once read: "Things work out in the end. If it hasn't worked out, it's not the end." So, until the end, keep your heart open and expect good things.

Have a Clear Heart

Beyond having an open heart, another essential aspect of self-love is to have a *clear* heart. If the open heart is that of your Divine inner child, consider the clear heart to be that of your Divine inner *adult*.

To have a clear heart means to step away from the confusion and fog of drama and self-pity and look at life without bias. A clear heart allows you to engage in life with objectivity and reason. When your heart is clear, you don't take life personally. When it's not, it's very difficult to love yourself, because you're too busy being victimized and abused by those around you . . . and suffering for it.

A client named Ted, utterly distraught, came to see me for a reading. His wife of ten years had recently undergone gastric-bypass surgery and lost 125 pounds. But rather than this being a good thing, she immediately started acting out her food addiction in other ways, taking up drinking and doing drugs in place of overeating. She went from being a stable—albeit obese—wife and mother to his two children to being a five-nights-a-week party animal who could barely find her way home at night because she was so wasted.

Ted felt beyond furious and betrayed. "I supported her surgery, I took care of the kids while she recovered, and I've been a great husband. How could she do this to us? To her kids? To *me?*"

His life was suddenly in shambles, and his suffering was palpable—but his heart wasn't clear, taking her behavior personally and internalizing it as a rejection of him or interpreting it as a failure on his part to be a good husband. After all, if he were good enough, she'd love him enough not to self-indulge, right? *Wrong.*

What Ted—with his cloudy, confused heart—utterly failed to understand even before his wife's gastric bypass was that she was a highly addicted, out-of-control woman whose behavior had nothing to do with him. Unless he could see that, his personalizing of her addictions only made it worse. He couldn't love himself, let alone his wife or children, until his heart cleared. Quite simply, her struggles weren't about him, and therefore he couldn't fix them—or her.

Fortunately, their struggles drew him into counseling, where slowly his heart began to clear. Then one day he said to me, "For the longest time, I resisted getting my heart cleared up about my wife's problems. I took some sort of sick pleasure in believing it had to do with me. What was that about?"

I *know* what that's about. I've done it myself—when I blamed myself for an ex-boyfriend's infidelity, for example, even though he had clearly demonstrated a pattern of cheating on past girlfriends. I've done it when I thought that I could make my husband happy by unsolicited suggestions that he change the direction of his career, only to get impatient and frustrated with him for not appreciating my "good" ideas. I've even done it when I was overzealous in assisting my oldest daughter in finding the right college, cramping her style and then feeling unappreciated when she resisted my help.

You can't get to a clear heart through the ego, because this part of you gets in the way and blocks the Spirit from taking you to higher ground. You must decide that you're not going to be a victim of anyone's behavior in order to access a clear heart. Once you do, your heart automatically begins to clear.

You begin to understand that your boss acts like a bully because he's insecure, not because you're doing a bad job. You recognize that your child is angry and defensive because he's neglecting his responsibilities and not because you're a bad parent. You see that your neighbor is curt and rude because she isn't feeling well and doesn't have adequate insurance, not because she resents you.

Having a clear heart is an enormously self-loving choice because it frees you from absorbing everyone else's misery and lets you enjoy your peace.

To have a clear heart is simple:

1. Take nothing personally. Whatever someone does or doesn't do isn't about *you.*

2. Don't be a victim. Remember that you can't control others, but you *can* choose how you respond to them.

Once Ted's heart cleared up, he chose to divorce his wife, seek counseling for himself, and assume full-time custody of the children. It was clearly the only road to the love of self, of his children, and, ironically, of his wife. When he stopped reacting and saw for the first time how profoundly she suffered from addictions, he found detachment from—and compassion for—her. They boxed out a fairly messy divorce, but even that he didn't take personally. Now that he's on the other side of his fiasco, he can also see how his own insecurities drew him to someone with addictions.

❁

A clear heart is a creative one. When yours is clear, you can see subtle connections and hidden relationships. You begin to understand what's really going on with people and can therefore make better choices about how you want to respond. You remove the chaos and drama that victimhood brings. With a clear heart, you take back your power to choose and create.

To clear your heart is simple. Just change the question from *Why is this happening to me?* to *Why is this happening? What's the relationship between cause and effect, choice and outcome?* or even better, *What can I learn from this?*

Study, rather than react . . . unplug from drama and breathe through your challenges with objectivity. This isn't to imply that you can't *feel* anything. Feelings are good and inform you about your choices. When you feel bad, there's something to learn. For example, if you feel depressed, you learn that you might need to take better care of your health or that you're ignoring your needs. If you feel angry, you learn that you're not respecting your boundaries and need to examine where you're letting others push you around. If you feel irritable or impatient, you learn that something that's going on is ungrounded and unclear or, perhaps, not truthful.

The benefits of a clear heart are many—it's the heart that reduces stress, improves vitality, and restores energy. The clearer *your* heart, the less draining life is. It's also the heart that empowers you and restores creativity. If your heart is clouded and confused, you can't find your way to a solution. You just spin around in "suffering" circles. Although self-dramatizing is seductive to your ego, it's actually a waste of time.

Nothing positive or good comes out of a clouded, confused heart; and nothing fogs it and interrupts your ability to self-love more quickly and thoroughly than fear. The minute you feel afraid, the heart clouds up and confusion sets in.

What I've discovered, however, is that we don't have to overcome fear to have a clear heart. We simply need to recognize it when it shows up and acknowledge its presence. The great revelation for me is that it isn't fear itself so much as the effort of hiding or denying it that's so self-abusive and destructive.

Being afraid is normal, especially when facing the unknown. For example, I remember the evening before I was to present a daylong workshop in Sydney, Australia. All day I had felt tense and anxious. I slept during the afternoon yet still found myself restless and slightly irritable. Then all of a sudden it occurred to me why I was feeling so out of sorts: I was afraid.

Once I acknowledged this, a whole constellation of fears unraveled. I was afraid . . .

- . . . that I wouldn't connect with the audience.

- . . . that I wouldn't be effective.

- . . . that my guidance wouldn't work well.

- . . . that the audience wouldn't respond to my music selection.

I was just afraid in general. The more I acknowledged my fears, the more they began to subside and the more clarity returned to my heart.

Once it did, my heart said: *Yes, any one of those things may happen. It's not likely, but it's possible. And so what if it does? It wouldn't be the end of the world.*

And that was true. It could possibly be uncomfortable, even unpleasant. Yet it wouldn't be anything more than a temporary slight to my ego if the worst indeed came to pass.

That thought made me laugh. So many of our fears really are nothing more than threats to our already-insecure egos. If we remember that we are Spirit, however, we get free of the ego's freak-outs. The more we simply acknowledge our fears with love and a dash of humor, the more they subside and "defog" the heart.

Now, there's a big difference between feeling vague, generic fear and actually being in danger. Most of the time when we experience fear, there's no threat to anything other than our fragile egos. But even when we *are* in danger, it's far better to acknowledge fear's presence so that our hearts will clear up and our guidance will come through to help get us out of it.

I recall once as a student in France, I accepted a ride home from a man I met at a party because it was late, the trains were no longer running, it was cold outside, and I had no money for a taxi. Stupid, I know, but I was young.

The minute I got in the car with him, I felt afraid, so I acknowledged this to myself. Once I did, my Spirit said, *You should be scared. This man has bad intentions.*

As soon as my guidance revealed that, I turned to the man and said, "Oh my goodness, I have to get out of the car now or I'm going to be sick all over the place."

The man was shocked, and suddenly I saw fear in his eyes. Noticing his expensive car and suit, I knew why.

When I started to get out, the fear subsided and relief took its place. I even laughed a little as I walked home, freezing but safe.

Whenever you feel afraid, acknowledge it, either out loud or to yourself. Be as specific as possible about what you fear. Say that you don't know why if you don't. Notice how the more you articulate your fear, the clearer your heart becomes. Once it's unclouded, ask your Spirit, *Is this a real or imagined threat?* Listen to the answer. If it's real, ask the clear heart to guide you quickly to safety; if it's imagined, ask it to step aside. The more often and more quickly you confront fear, the sooner your heart will be clear and remain so. And a clear heart is a self-loving one, because only *it* can see and guide you creatively to a solution.

What fogs and disturbs a clear heart are strong emotions of any sort. Whether intense anger, strong infatuation, overwhelming grief, or unbelievable ecstasy, powerful waves of emotion temporarily distort the clarity of the heart and interrupt our ability to love ourselves or others.

This isn't to suggest that we must attempt to block or distance ourselves from our emotions. Not at all. In fact, blocked emotions close and clog the heart and shut it down altogether. No, it's important to feel all of our emotions fully and completely and to recognize them for the messengers they are, informing us about the experiences of our lives. It's just that we need to recognize that our emotions are like the weather: They come and—ideally, if unblocked—they go. We learn from them but shouldn't *act* on them. It's best to wait until their intensity passes, then choose our actions.

For example, I have a client named Sally who's a passionate, creative woman with a brilliant Spirit and a volatile temper. On several occasions, she found herself losing her cool with her husband and, in the midst of the battle, telling him that she wanted a divorce. Once her rage passed and her heart was clear, she had no desire to end the marriage, and in fact most of her outbursts had little to do with her husband at all. Sadly, he didn't know this, and after one declaration of divorce too many, he left her and *did* file for divorce. Her distorted heart failed to recognize how painful her outbursts were to her husband. He refused to stay with her—his own heart had shut down.

Had she simply waited long enough to let her waves of anger pass rather than acting on them, she might still be married. Her impulsive utterances were Sally's undoing and hurt her more than anyone.

The same held true for another client, George, who lost his wife of 35 years and found himself overwhelmed by grief and loneliness. While in the midst of sorrow, he met a woman who had newly emigrated from Bulgaria. Impulsively, he asked her to marry him, and she agreed. He knew that his heart wasn't clear and that it was a bad idea, but he acted anyway. The infatuation wore off in less than three months, and resentment took its place. Not surprisingly, after battling for three years, they divorced. Now he had that disaster to add to his still-unresolved grief.

Let your emotions rise and fall and learn from them, but don't let them guide you in life. Whenever you find yourself caught in the turbulence of a strong emotion, let it flow and know that it will eventually calm down. You're best able to make sound, self-loving choices when your emotions are quiet.

To help calm them, channel their expression in benign, healthy ways. Journaling is a wonderfully effective way to harness strong emotions and help you regain balance . . . so is walking, running, talking with a neutral friend, going to the gym, pummeling a punching bag, dancing, taking a long hot shower, screaming into a pillow, or shouting into the wind at the beach.

Express your emotions—just don't *act* on them. Whether they're good or bad, wait until they're clear before you arrive at any decisions. This, of course, takes discipline, especially if you're a passionate person. Yet if you think about it, some of the worst, most unloving choices you've ever made probably have come about while you were worked up. It's in the throes of strong emotion that you're most critical and judgmental of yourself and everyone around you.

When your heart is clear, you can feel your Spirit and automatically find great love and appreciation for yourself. But when it isn't, you can't touch or sense your Spirit because your ego is freaking out. Know that emotion passes. Be patient and let it do so, like rolling thunderclouds across the sky. When your heart is clear, it's much easier to make healthy, self-loving choices that honor your Spirit.

Have a Wise Heart

To love yourself, you must find peace. And the way to peace is through the wise heart.

The wise heart is that of your ancient soul, engaging reason and connecting choices and behaviors with consequences and outcomes. It's the universal heart—the aspect of self-love that moves away from the personal "I" and sees you as part of a greater whole, the human race. The wise heart encourages you to move beyond personal gain and begin to consider the impact of each of your choices on the whole of humanity. This is the heart of self-control on an ego level—the heart that opts not to drink and drive, that refrains from overspending through credit cards, and that chooses fresh food over fast food when planning meals. It's the heart that uses energy-saving lightbulbs.

The wise heart is the one that cares about the consequences of your choices. This aspect of self-love is extremely underutilized in most people, especially in Western cultures. It's far more popular and seductive to posture and swagger, acceding to the demands of the ego, than to be forward-thinking and wise.

The opposite of the wise heart is the foolish heart, which *re*acts rather than *acts* in life. This is the heart that surrenders all genuine personal spiritual power over to the whims and adrenaline of the moment, only to regret those same self-righteous choices and selfish behaviors later. It's the heart of overreaction.

I learned (accidentally) to engage the wise heart when I was about ten years old. Walking home alone from school one day, I encountered a group of public-school kids who taunted and teased me for being the "Catholic girl in the stupid uniform."

Embarrassed, afraid, and outnumbered, I didn't know quite what to do. My fearful self wanted to cry. My instinctive self wanted to run. My courageous self wanted to fight back. Yet my higher self even then knew that none of these options would serve to protect me or get me out of the predicament I had fallen into. The only option left was to be quiet and do nothing—in other words, not to react.

I looked my tormenters right in the eye as they heckled me, but held a neutral expression. I revealed neither fear nor anger, much the way my older brother often looked at me when I taunted him. To my surprise, it worked: My neutrality and absence of reaction disarmed them. In a matter of less than five minutes, they became bored with their game and moved on. I stood immobile for a few more moments as the pack began to drift away, then I continued slowly on my route—or at least until I turned the corner and was out of their sight. Then I ran the rest of the way home as fast as I could.

The first person I encountered when I arrived home was the very same older brother I often attempted to torment. He listened dispassionately as I spilled the details of my frightening story, telling him how I refused to react or show my fear and how, to my surprise, the other kids eventually moved on.

His only response was: "That was wise," and then he, too, sauntered away. Thinking it over, he was right. It *was* wise to hold my tongue, to look them in the eye, and to wait it out rather than react. And it wasn't something I normally did. In the midst of the threat, I accessed a wisdom that I didn't know I had. And that wisdom spared me from a number of possible unpleasant outcomes—it saved me from harm.

Since then, I've often thought about wisdom and how it protects and serves us in all situations. One thing I've learned is that in order to access it, we need to forfeit the need to be "right." The minute we believe we're "right," someone else must inevitably be "wrong." And as long as there's "right" versus "wrong," there will be conflict.

This isn't to say that you shouldn't have morals, values, and convictions and stick to them. It just means that what *you* feel is right isn't necessarily what feels right to someone else. Respect these differences in opinion and perspective. While it's important to live with your inner morals and guidance, it's not loving to impose them on others—especially by the use of force—and doing so will bring only harm.

Having wisdom means developing a respectful sensitivity and clear understanding of other people's rights, too. Simply put, "Do unto others as you would have them do unto you." That's it.

To be wise means to bite your tongue, bide your time, forgive the moment, and respond to a difficult or infuriating situation with love rather than fear or anger. Having a wise heart entails being in control of your passion, instead of allowing *it* to control *you*. It means channeling your aggression or passive aggression into thoughtful actions rather than being enslaved by your reactions. Engaging the wise heart asks you to embrace the old adage "This, too, shall pass" and choose to live in the peace and calm that comes from using your higher reason, as opposed to constantly facing the damage control that hotheaded emotional reaction necessitates.

❀

Engaging a wise heart is more than simply controlling your emotions—it's also accessing higher reason to guide you through tough situations.

Betty engaged her wise heart when she divorced her cheating husband, Edward, after 13 years of marriage. Even though she was enraged by his transgressions and at times wanted to hurt him for the hurt he caused her, their seven-year-old twins adored their father, and Betty didn't want to destroy their world or their relationship with him. So, as difficult as it was for her, Betty acted wisely: She forgave her husband for his betrayal and never spoke an unkind word to or about him in front of their children during the divorce proceedings and afterward. She held her feelings in check and only shared them with her therapist. She exerted extreme self-control out of love for her kids and a desire for her own peace.

Edward, in contrast, tried to justify his behavior by attacking Betty. Then he attempted to minimize his actions by giving her excuses and blaming her. Next came gifts and promises. She steadfastly refused to react. He then distanced himself from her and became confrontational and argumentative. Still, she remained calmly and wisely detached. She simply said, "I love you as a person, Edward, but I no longer choose to be your wife."

After two years of this conduct, their divorce was finalized. In the midst of it, Edward asked Betty for forgiveness, and she gave it to him. In the end, they actually became genuine friends. As a result of Betty's wisdom, Edward stopped attacking her, blaming her, and feeling ashamed of his actions and simply admitted that he'd been too immature to be a good husband.

During this time, Betty realized that she had been too controlling to be in a healthy partnership, especially with someone so immature. To be so controlling left little opportunity for her spouse to have much genuine influence over the marriage. She learned to step back, admit her vulnerabilities, and allow others to be there for her. This all took a lot of honest emotional work on her part, but it was worth it.

After the divorce, Edward moved a block away from Betty and stayed closely involved with, and committed to, his sons. Betty continued therapy and remarried a far more mature man five years later. Edward and the new husband eventually became friends, and now they all vacation together.

This was only made possible by Betty's ability to be wise throughout her divorce rather than "right." She looked at the bigger picture in lieu of righteously choosing to be "wronged" and battle it out with Edward or punish him for her pain.

The way to engage our own wise heart is through prayer and faith. To do so, we need to give up control and surrender our personal will and perspective over to the Divine. Wisdom is a spiritual gift that lies in all hearts, waiting to be activated. We must step back from our egos and consciously engage our timeless higher selves. Wisdom is rooted in the remembrance that, in the end, all lives come and go; all things on the human plane have a beginning, middle, and end; and it's only what serves the Spirit that lasts in the long run. Wisdom is the knowledge that only those choices in life that bring us closer to God and Divine mind are of any value. Those that take us away from Divine mind are harmful—not only to us, but to everyone.

Every day we're given chances to be a little wiser than the day before. They come when someone cuts us off in traffic, disrespects or disrupts our plans, or robs us of our peace. These opportunities to be wise are inherent every time someone doesn't do what we want them to do.

You can be foolish and react with negativity, have an emotional outburst, or vent your uncontrolled indignation, but this won't change the other person and only makes you look ridiculous and feel enraged. Not only does being foolish not give you what you want, a foolish heart makes things worse. It causes you to act before you think, lash out before considering the effects, and become so invested in being right that you sacrifice all hope for peace and tranquility for a temporary moment of control.

A client recently asked me how to best develop a wise heart. She did so because she was married but in love with someone else. She liked her husband and didn't want a divorce but felt deeply drawn to the other man. She didn't know how to remain connected to him and still be faithfully married. My answer was: "Do what you can live with—do what brings you peace."

Thinking this over, she decided that she couldn't live with a secret affair, but did want to have the man she loved in her life. Her wise decision was to introduce him to her husband, curb her sexual attraction, and enjoy him as a friend. Eventually her husband and the other man became best friends, allowing all three of them to coexist peacefully.

❀

Where in your life are you presently exercising a wise heart? It might be in choosing to overlook the road rager cutting across your path. It might be ignoring your teenager's rude remarks rather than picking a fight. It might be not responding to someone's uncalled-for criticism as opposed to sniping back.

What choices bring you peace? It might be tolerating your co-workers' mistakes rather than getting upset. It could be listening to your parents without being defensive, choosing to respect their point of view even if you don't agree with it.

What behaviors leave you feeling content with yourself? Perhaps it's giving up a personal perspective to accommodate the group idea, or forgiving someone who has let you down and not taking it personally. It might be listening to another's complaint without being defensive or reactive. . . . Those are the expressions of your wise heart.

Alternatively, where in your life do you lack peace? Where do you serve your pride in its place? When do you blame, lash out, condemn, or refuse to apologize or forgive, preferring righteous indignation instead? Where are you consistently shortsighted, quick-tempered, close-minded, and self-indulgent? These are costly decisions that rob you of the foundations of self-love, which are self-esteem and inner peace.

The wise heart is that of your inner elder, your ancient one. It's the aspect of your Spirit that knows that as time passes, emotions calm, passions subside, and clarity returns. The wise heart merges reason with emotion so that your response is both wholehearted *and* whole-brained. It engages all of your faculties—feeling and thought, passion and reason—and discerns a course of action that benefits everyone, not just you.

A wise heart feels passionately but acts with prudence. It leads you to discernment and patience. The wise heart springs not only from your highest personal reason, but also from the wisdom of the ages—a gift from your ancestors, anchored in your DNA.

Another source of wisdom available to us is the wisdom of humankind. It's the collective learning we can all draw from as human beings. All wisdom is the legacy our predecessors passed on to us. It's a gift derived from their pain, their anguish, and their mistakes—as well as their victories—one that's made available to spare us suffering.

To access ancient wisdom, call upon your ancestors, both personal and collective. Ask yourself what wisdom they've passed on. Give this real thought.

I have a neighbor who comes from a stubborn, prideful Sicilian family. The wisdom he gained from them is that of loyalty, steadfast commitment, and endurance. But he has also gleaned wisdom from their mistakes, by watching the pain their suspicions and narrow-mindedness cost them. He saw how they'd rather suffer than allow others to help them. Observing their mistakes, he's wise enough to judge less quickly, trust more easily, and let others in. Their experiences enlightened him.

One of the wisest things we can do is learn from our ancestors. We can study the past, both good and bad, and take the lessons of our forebears to heart.

The wise heart in all of us sees the continuity of life. It understands cycles and observes how life keeps coming back to itself again and again. If we're wise, we slow down, connect the dots, observe and learn from others, study cause and effect, and choose to be peaceful over being right. *Right* is the subjective reaction of the fleeting ego. *Peace* is a universal response to the deepest Spirit.

Have a Courageous Heart

The courageous heart is the aspect of your authentic Spirit that sticks to your convictions, stands true in the face of fear rather than running away or becoming unconscious, and cherishes *self*-approval over the approval of others.

The courageous heart endows you with the ability to say no when you must; stick up for what you believe in; and face off attack without giving in or acquiescing to what goes against your principles, morals, ethics, or values. It is the heart of strength, and no one can fully self-love and live their Spirit if they lack one.

The courageous heart is the fiery heart. It's the one that not only feels what's true for our Spirit, but that acts on our feelings. In my 35 years of private practice as an intuitive consultant, I've rarely met a person who told me that he or she didn't sense what was right for his or her Spirit. As Divine Beings, we *do* feel what's right. That's not enough, however. We must also *act on* what our Spirit suggests to truly live the love our Spirit conveys.

I just finished teaching a small class in Chicago devoted to this very topic. When I asked the students how many acted on what their Spirit suggested—such as contacting a new person they were attracted to, starting a creative project, initiating a change of job, or changing their direction in a health matter—fewer than half raised their hands. When I asked why, the answer was universally because they were afraid. It seemed that they were waiting to feel safe enough, secure enough. No matter how much love, approval, affection, security, or calming peace you provide the ego, it will *never* be enough. The ego wants absolute control of everything outside of itself, and that can never be achieved.

❁

Several years ago while on a trip to South Africa, I received a lesson on the courageous heart that changed my life forever. Shortly after completing several work-shops in Johannesburg, Durban, and Cape Town, I rewarded myself with the gift of a three-day safari in the South African bush.

First I flew on a commercial aircraft for an hour from Johannesburg to a distant point, then took yet another, smaller aircraft an additional 20 minutes to an absolutely remote landing strip, and finally drove another hour to a tiny camp where the safari began.

Just being a guest in this vast experience of nature was a miracle, especially for me, the city girl from Chicago. The days ran from 3:30 A.M. till 7:30 A.M., driving around the bush sighting animals, and resumed again from 4:00 P.M. to around 7:00 P.M. Everything I saw was extraordinary: The hyenas, elephants, rhinoceroses, and giraffes, all in their natural elements, were breathtaking.

On the last evening, just after the sun had completely set and we were about to return to camp, there was a flurry of radio chatter between my driver and those of several other Range Rovers in the area. Something remarkable had been sighted.

We all rushed in our vehicles to the same spot, where we parked and waited in silence. The guides gave us no indication of what we were waiting for. We just peered into the dark and watched. Suddenly, out of the bush emerged a mother lion leading her five cubs to water. Seeing them took my breath away. The minute they were near, all the Range Rovers flashed their bright headlights right at them, yet neither mother nor cubs even so much as acknowledged our presence. Instead, the mother, keeping her attention on her goal of leading her cubs, padded steadily along without shifting her gaze to the left or the right even once.

When she passed our Range Rover, she was so close to me that I could feel and smell her hot breath and notice the deep scars in her face from past battles. Goose bumps jumped all over my flesh as she slunk by. I noticed something else as well: her powerful, unwavering, fearless intention—so formidable that it held her five cubs at absolute attention as she proceeded with her objective. It was a vibration of such clarity, purpose, and commitment that nothing would dare interrupt her flow. As she passed, I suddenly embodied what it vibrationally meant to be "lionhearted."

To have courage of this magnitude only comes with unwavering focus, and commitment to what the Spirit requires. The lions needed water to live, and they were going to get it. Nothing would disturb this . . . and nothing dared. They were fearless in their intention.

I thought of others similarly fearless in their intentions—Gandhi, Nelson Mandela, Mother Teresa, Joan of Arc—and suddenly realized that we all could be part of the brother- and sisterhood of courageous hearts. All it takes is unwavering focus on our goal. The courageous heart sets its course and doesn't ask in fear and doubt how it will achieve its goals. The hows reveal themselves as the process unfolds.

Nelson Mandela didn't know how to end apartheid, but his heart was *convinced* that he would. Mother Teresa didn't know how she would care for so many desperate people, but she *decided* she would. Gandhi didn't know how he would free India from British rule—the *how* wasn't his primary focus; that it *would* occur was his only concern.

When your head, heart, and feet align with higher intentions, God and all of nature align with *you* as well.

You create a seamless vibration of power and protection. When you become lionhearted, you love yourself and live your Spirit. You summon the Divine flame of God, fill your heart with courage, ignore your ego's fears and your need to control, and choose to be true to yourself no matter what.

Courage is the heart of action, not hesitation.

- It's the heart that my client Jenny demonstrated when she suddenly dropped out of business school and enrolled in a design program, even though her friends and family protested, "What a waste!"

- It's the heart of John when he chose not to sue the woman who withdrew her contract to buy his house when friends and lawyers alike cried "fraud" and encouraged the battle.

- It's the heart of the young child who smiles and greets the homeless man instead of blankly looking the other way.

To live our Spirit requires the spunk and fire of courage. We all have a lion heart within. And even if we feel like the Cowardly Lion in *The Wizard of Oz* at times, we must still stay the course.

Be afraid, but don't quit. Be worried, but don't quit. Be nervous, but don't quit. Steadfastly, like the mother lion in the bush, just keep placing one foot in front of the other, with your eye on the goal. Don't indulge your fearful ego's whys and hows. Trust and keep steady and

your Spirit will reveal the way as you proceed. That's
your Divine agreement.

❊　❊　❊

STEP 6

Share Your Gifts

Simple Lesson: Share Your Gifts

This step aims at making you aware of the beautiful gifts your Spirit brings to this world. The practice that follows encourages creativity as the most direct way to experience your true sense of purpose. You'll discover the richness of Spirit in all creative endeavors and develop greater confidence in your personal contributions to life.

❁

Embedded in the heart of every soul born on this earth is a huge basket filled with gifts that it wishes to share with the world. Some of those gifts are obvious, and others are less so. However, each—no matter what it is—is an equally important contribution to the balance and joy of the world and is necessary to the whole.

On a deep level, we feel the treasures lodged deep within our hearts, waiting to be discovered and shared. Intuitively, we know that we have something we must contribute in order to feel at peace with ourselves and be of service to the world. We call this longing to contribute our "purpose," and we spend vast amounts of time and energy seeking to find out exactly what that purpose is.

The answer is simple: Our purpose is to look deeply into our hearts and share what we love. We are simply to open our interior gift basket and then uncover and share those things that bring us great personal joy. That's it.

The ego mind doesn't want this to be our purpose. It's too easy for its tastes, and only involves the heart. If the ego isn't involved, it loses power and must step back—which, as we know, it doesn't want to do. So to preserve its own interests, the ego distracts us and derides, minimizes, and criticizes the things we love, dismissing them as meaningless. We set off on a wild-goose chase to "save the world"—only, to validate the ego, we must get *paid* for our efforts as well.

Purpose is the simple sharing of Spirit that occurs when *your* heart opens wide enough in personal joy to activate those of others. Purpose lies in the everyday joy-filled, loving acts of caring and sharing that come directly from the heart and weave us all together as one family. Purpose isn't a profession—it can be *expressed* in your profession, but it doesn't have to *be* it, and often isn't.

I have a friend who had a nervous breakdown and suffered clinical depression in his early 30s. Since then, he has been unable to hold down anything other than a few odd jobs. At 63, he hasn't been a paid professional or employee anywhere in more than 30 years . . . and yet he is completely fulfilling his purpose.

The way he does this is by selflessly and quietly walking around the neighborhood being a good neighbor to those around him. He does simple things, such as getting out the hose to water the lawn or cutting the grass—not only at *his* house, but at his neighbors' as well, especially when they're out of town. In the winter, he trades in the lawn mower for a snow shovel and clears the sidewalks of snow and ice, making way for pedestrians to make it to the bus stop or train station to get to work.

He dabbles in the kitchen and frequently cooks up batches of cookies or bakes multilayered cakes. Then he randomly shows up at various other homes with a slice or two of cake or a few hot cookies in hand, along with an invitation for the neighbor to take a break and share a cup of coffee with him for a few minutes.

He loves to tinker with electronics as well, so he shows up to help with the latest TiVo installation, fix the short in the telephone line, or put in a new switch on the garbage disposal or washing machine so that no one has to call the service technician.

Is he doing all of this out of a sense of duty? Absolutely not. He simply does these things because he *loves* doing them. If you asked him whether he thought he was fulfilling his purpose through his actions, I'm certain he would say "Probably not," since he doesn't have a paying job.

Yet if you pose the same question to his neighbors and friends, they would respond quite differently. "He absolutely is fulfilling his purpose!" they would affirm. With his joyful, low-key contributions, he has transformed an impersonal city neighborhood into a place of belonging and community for all those he has touched over the years. He has more than fulfilled his purpose by simply sharing his gift of being a good neighbor and friend.

This brings to mind a woman who had been consulting with me for years, tortured about being unable to find or feel her purpose. While she, too, was a good friend, family member, and neighbor, her ego mind had her absolutely convinced that she'd wasted her life because her job as a secretary at an automobile dealership was utterly shameful in terms of its value.

Granted, the job itself hadn't been particularly rewarding or terribly fulfilling, but her steady work had allowed her to be the primary breadwinner for her family, including three children, since her husband had had a stroke at 37 and had been unable to fully function ever since.

Her gift was her ability to pick up the slack, be consistent, provide stability, and do it all with love and good-naturedness until the very last of her children graduated from college. Her purpose and love was holding the family intact, especially after her kids suffered the loss of an able-bodied father. Her job was secondary to her purpose. She said that she would have gladly cleaned toilets, cleared sewers, and scrubbed on her hands and knees if doing so was necessary, as long as this allowed her family to meet its basic financial needs, kept the kids at home, and permitted her husband to heal.

The entire time her children were growing up, she never even pondered the idea of purpose. She was too *engaged* in it to wonder about it. But once her kids were grown, her husband was relatively stable, and the extreme stress was subsiding, her ego began to taunt her, telling her that she'd missed out on her life. Cruel, yes, but egos tend to be that way.

In our last session, she felt rather desperate, no longer young or full of energy, and alone with herself. She asked, "What is my purpose?"

When I said that it was serving her heart, which in her case was the family, she seemed skeptical. "My kids are grown up and gone now," she lamented. "Does this mean my purpose is over?"

"Not at all," I replied. "It's just evolving. You served the family in hard times, which you loved. Now practice serving in *good* times. Celebrate your togetherness now—encourage relaxation and discussions . . . even plan outings.

"Your purpose was to keep the family grounded and intact financially. Now that purpose can evolve into keeping the family grounded and intact *emotionally.* Call your kids. Be concerned with who they've become, and communicate with them. Take an interest in them as adults and enjoy them. That's your purpose for now."

She remained suspicious. "You mean I don't have to personally stop the genocide in Darfur or 'leave no child behind' in school?"

"Of course you can campaign for those issues if they speak to your heart," I replied. "But maintaining a loving, positive connection with your own children is just as important."

She was quiet. "Well, that's what I love most," she mused. "That seems almost too easy."

"That's your ego talking. Listen to your heart now. What does *it* say?"

Again, she was quiet. After a moment, she spoke: "My heart says to relax. I've been attending to my life with love, so I've been doing the right thing for me."

"Exactly," I answered.

Purpose isn't complicated. It's not what you do that constitutes fulfillment—it's that whatever you do, you do it because you love it and therefore are *loving* when you do it.

I have a friend who sells old clothing and junk on eBay, and she's having the time of her life. She's in purpose mode because in her energetic recycling endeavors, she's having fun and infusing joy into the lives of those she touches. Her buyers have fun as well. The wheel of "stuff" goes 'round and 'round, but in the end all are satisfied. The result is a positive vibration that touches everyone.

Be very suspicious of your ego if it suggests to you that unless you're single-handedly executing some heroic, selfless feat, you're missing your purpose. A telltale clue that your ego is at work is the pressure it puts on you to do something "significant." Any feeling or thought floating through your mind that you must do or be something special in order to fulfill your true purpose should be laughed at and exposed for what it is: a narcissistic ego trip.

The Spirit never demands to be or do something special. It only encourages you to be and do what you love. It's not so much the action itself that makes something purposeful as it is the *vibration* that the action creates. If it creates a loving one, continue. If not, stop and re-examine what you're doing.

For example, I had a client in Chicago who was obsessed with finding her purpose. A freelance writer covering what she called "meaningless yuppie materialism," she was angry with—and judgmental of—herself and impatient with the way her life was unfolding, so she quit writing and turned to volunteer work.

During the period between the time she enrolled and the time she was actually assigned work, her ego stopped harassing her. Instead, it strutted around like a peacock with its tail spread. At last she could say what she was doing mattered . . . she could, that is, until she received her assignment.

Instead of saving Africa from AIDS, she was assigned to run a small mobile library in rural Texas. There was no glamour, no excitement, and no romance in this. It was only tedious, fairly boring work serving a poor community overrun with alcohol and methamphetamine abuse. She was appalled and disgusted. In spite of how loudly her ego crowed over her selflessness, her heart remained uninspired. In fact, just the opposite was true: She despised every minute of it and, sadly, hated the people she met as well. They were disinterested, unmotivated, and generally couldn't care less about reading, leaving her angry and frustrated.

Nevertheless, she put in her two years, not only miserable herself, but causing the already-miserable people around her even more misery as well.

Oh well, such are the diversions of the ego.

When we last spoke, she shook her head and said, "I was certain that was my purpose. It sure *sounded* good, anyway."

It wasn't. Now she runs a small bath-and-body shop in a friendly Chicago neighborhood and writes kids' stories. No longer an angry, resentful volunteer, she organizes a children's story hour in her neighborhood bookstore, publishes her own books, and feels that in her own small way she's adding to the joy of the world.

The point of all of this is that purpose can't be found outside you. Rather, it can only be found by opening your heart, connecting to what you love, and sharing with others. In the great equation of life, if we each pursue our purpose, all of our needs will be met.

Before you arrived, you and God had a talk and you hand-selected your gifts together. None is any more or less valuable than any other. In the Divine realm, if it comes from love and is shared with love, the gift is triumphant.

Your gift may be creating music, solving great mathematical equations, discovering new biofuels, reading stories to babies, mowing the lawn, or picking up garbage. The ego differentiates these things as more or less important, but not the Spirit. The Divine mind knows that all that comes from love is important, and every loving act contributes to the whole.

All gifts are equal in Divine mind. Claiming, valuing, and then sharing yours completely, without hesitation or interference from your ego, is one of the greatest and simplest secrets to loving yourself and living your Spirit.

What do *you* love? Sharing that fully is your purpose.

Simple Practice: Create

The highest, most joyful expression of the Divine Spirit within comes through creativity. Nothing is more powerful. Nothing is more self-loving. And nothing is more rewarding. It doesn't matter what you create, as long as it makes your life more beautiful and satisfying, because *all* creativity is the Holy Spirit in action.

The ego mind doesn't create; only the Spirit within creates. The only thing that the ego mind manifests is drama and frustration, leaving you and everyone around you depleted, exhausted, and miserable. Drama is the cheap, impotent substitute for true creative expression: You can tell whether you're creating in the beautiful frequency of Divine mind or are swallowed up by the frequency of ego mind by the amount of it in your life.

For example, if you find yourself having frequent arguments with significant others, often feel angry and mistreated at work, spend vast amounts of time ruminating over comments others have made—or didn't make, get easily offended, cause discord or get upset with others, and often announce how you have no choice and must simply suffer life as it is, you're in drama. The same holds true if you overreact to change or spend time resenting the way things are or fearing the way they might be. If you dwell on the question *What's wrong with this picture?* instead of focusing on what's right, you're in drama.

Culturally we've been scared away from our creativity by what my dear friend Julia Cameron, the author of *The Artist's Way,* calls *creativity monsters*—the voices from the past and present who criticize, attack, ridicule, and judge us, and who banish us from owning and expressing our creativity with joy and abandon.

They're the art teachers who gave your work low grades, the music teachers who told you that you couldn't sing or play a tune, the friends who laughed at your dance moves, or the coach who wouldn't allow you to perform in the all-school talent show. They're the people who imply that creativity must be "good" in order to be valuable, who subject your work to public appraisal before you're allowed to join the club.

These creativity monsters forget that creativity is the highest Divine right bestowed upon us all, and our creations are the voice and expression of our Spirit. Without creativity grounded in our daily lives as a personal resource of joy and renewal, our Spirits are muffled, muted, and denied

If we don't allow ourselves to express ourselves creatively, we can't live our Spirit. Being creative is one of the fundamental ways in which we do love ourselves and live our Spirit, and being creative will always succeed in bringing that love and life force forward.

One of the problems that distances so many of us from our creative Spirit is the notion that being creative is synonymous with being a professional or an aspiring artist. It's not. It simply means making something new out of something that presently exists.

Being creative can be as simple as baking a cake; making a flower arrangement; rearranging the furniture in your living room; or trying out a new outfit, haircut, or color. It can be as uncomplicated as writing a poem, making up new words to a song, solving a crossword puzzle, or fixing a broken window yourself. There are so many ways to be creative that it's impossible to name them all. Mostly, though, it means tapping into your inventive, beauty-oriented, loving Spirit and allowing it to come out and play for a while.

My daughter Sabrina, like her father, is highly creative in the kitchen. A lover of sweets but possessing a sugar and wheat intolerance, she never ceases to amaze all of us with her sugar- and gluten-free pastries, cakes, and pies. She doesn't even follow recipes. She just experiments and sees what happens. Some of her culinary creations are delicious. Some are . . . well, let's say, *interesting* and not necessarily edible, but still fulfilling and fun for her to invent.

Every time she's stressed with school or overworked in the thinking department, we can be sure to find her in the kitchen, apron on, whizzing around like a mad chemist, conjuring up yet another guilt-free treat.

My other daughter is completely different. Always having been passionate about music, she expresses her creativity by making CD compilations of great recording artists, either for herself or her friends. This endeavor occupies her for hours at a time, but she always emerges with a great mix and a heart full of light.

I have a neighbor whose creative love is tinkering in the backyard. Armed with tools and a cheap radio, he spends hours rewiring old lamps, sanding doors, fixing stereos or vacuum cleaners, or dabbing paint on the house trim. When his partner of 41 years passed away several years ago, he thought that he'd die of grief right alongside her. The tinkering saved him. It paced his mourning and gave his Spirit respites of peace and calm. When overwhelmed, he'd wander out back and begin what he called a "mindless" project. He was accurate: Creativity relieves us of our ego minds and parks us squarely in the calm of our Spirit.

My mother not only encouraged creativity as a way for us to love ourselves and live our Spirit, she used it as a method of communicating directly with her higher self and with Divine wisdom. Her outlets were several, but centered on photography, oil painting, and sewing.

As a mother of seven children, all born close together, with my father's aging parents to care for, she found that it was easy for her ego to get flustered and become quite upset at times. When this occurred, she would excuse herself and go to her darkroom, studio, or sewing room with a stern warning to us not to bother her. And we didn't. But we did love when she retreated because while she often exited in a tizzy, she always returned in a good mood.

In the quiet efforts of sewing, developing photos, or painting, her concentration was so deep that her mind chatter quieted down. In the silence, she often heard her inner voice loud and clear, offering comfort, guidance, suggestions, and direction. She developed stronger-than-ever powers of intuition in these long, quiet sessions of simply being creative.

My husband, Patrick, is highly energetic by nature, which at times can make it difficult for him to calm down. The creative effort he naturally gravitates toward during more stressful periods is work in the garden. Whether he's pulling weeds, planting flowers, laying brick borders, or arranging flower boxes, he gets quiet and relaxes.

Sometimes when he's restless, his ego has been known to start trouble, just to get things stirred up because he's bored. He becomes argumentative and controlling, sticks his nose in where it doesn't belong, and offers opinions no one wants to hear. Early in our marriage this drove me nuts. I thought that he was just a troublemaker. Although it took a while, I eventually saw through the surface of his behavior and recognized that all this drama was being stirred up because he didn't know that he needed to be creative. Once I pegged the issue, I knew what to do. Rather than fighting it, I redirected it.

I bought him paints, brushes, and canvases for Christmas. I asked him to make us holiday cards, write poems for my Website, and cook gourmet meals for dinner. And he did. The minute he engaged his creative Spirit, the drama stopped and he was happy.

Many who have suffered life's atrocities have found a saving grace in their creativity. I once knew a woman named Lydia who had lived in Bulgaria, where she suffered many social, emotional, and political indignities while the country was under a Communist regime. Yet, although she lost much and had little, she was able to knit. And knit she did—so well, in fact, that she became a master. Eventually she moved to Canada with no more than the clothes on her back and her knitting needles.

It was slow at first, but soon Lydia had those needles clicking away for hours a day. Her work was so beautiful that she sold her creations instantly. In two short years, she had her own shop and two employees. She sold her wares and taught classes. "It's my love to create something beautiful," she told me when I met her at a workshop in Toronto. "I was born rich with my ability to create."

Wow! Now that was a Spirited comment. And her beaming smile also attested to her Spirit.

My grandmother—my father's mother, Antonia, who died when I was five years old—was very creative and filled with joy. She cooked, sewed, sang, danced, decorated, and celebrated. Because she was so creative, she was confident. Rather than fear or suffer deprivation, she used her creativity to look for a way to fill the lack. And she found it.

My mother was only 15 when she came to America, and Grandmother Antonia took her under her wing. "It was your grandmother," my mother told me, "who taught me to be so creative. She said that it was the secret to happiness, and God gave everyone the gift of creativity to keep us entertained. 'If you aren't creative,' she said to me, 'it's underused imagination and maybe a dose of self-pity, but it's *never* a lack of ability. We are all creative.'"

My mother took my grandmother's philosophy and creative example to heart. She raised us with the mantra: *No matter what problem you meet in life, simply know that there is always a solution.*

I believed her. When I was seven or eight, I wanted a pair of summer sandals, yet money was tight, so they were simply not in the budget. At first I was frustrated. I even threw a tantrum and cried to see if that would get me what I wanted. It didn't.

Observing my misery, my older brother Stefan walked over to me and calmly said, "You won't get sandals that way, so you might as well stop because no one is listening. Why don't you make a pair instead?"

"How?" I asked, wiping my tears.

"I dunno," he answered. "Figure it out." Then he walked away.

That was a thought. Maybe I could. I engaged my brother Bruce, always the engineer, and we set to work. We found some cardboard, old rope, and duct tape and were off. We spent nearly three days trying to perfect our model and finally succeeded. I emerged with a pair of cardboard-soled sandals with rope poking through the bottom—wrapped around my feet and then duct-taped on for stability. Never mind that I couldn't take them off. I didn't want to. I wore them for a week uninterrupted. I slept in them; I took my bath in them, feet sticking out of the water; and I walked all over the neighborhood showing them off. I was proud of those puppies.

Several weeks later my mom tapped me on the shoulder and said, "Come on, we're going to Montgomery Ward's."

"Why?" I asked, incredulous.

"To get you some real sandals." She smiled.

"But I like *my* sandals," I retorted. "I don't want new ones."

We were both surprised: she, because she thought I'd jump at the chance to get new sandals; me, because the ones I created made me so happy. So we went for a root-beer float instead.

Creating is an essential yet very simple tool for loving yourself and living your Spirit. Anytime you feel the disturbed energies of your ego mind blurring your joy, stop whatever you're doing, if possible, and try something creative.

The most important thing is to think: *I am creative.* To do so is to commune with Divine mind. To think *I am creative* is to align with the Spirit and solution, rather than the ego and problem.

Make it a Spiritual practice—or in other words, an exercise of Spirit—to be creative every day. People who have hobbies know the value of this. These diversions are daily touchstones of Spirit. You don't have to be Picasso. You don't have to be "good" at your creative endeavor. It's not for others to judge . . . it's for you to *enjoy.* So do.

❀   ❀   ❀

STEP 7

Remember
What You Love

Simple Lesson: Remember What You Love

This step aims to help you remember your Spirit and consciously connect to the beauty and joy that it exudes. The practice that follows introduces you to the joyful song of your Spirit, and immediately lifts the heavy burden of ego off your shoulders. You'll once again delight in yourself and all of life.

❁

One Saturday evening we threw a party to celebrate several family birthdays at once. Since they were milestone birthdays, we decided to go all out for the event. We rented tables, hired a caterer, and asked a neighbor who owns Chicago's top nightclub to serve as our DJ. Then we invited everyone we knew, ages 7 to 87, to join us . . . and we had a blast.

After dinner, the tables were removed, speakers were assembled, and our living room instantly became a disco.

A friend named Terry brought his 83-year-old father, George; and George's 78-year-old girlfriend, Thea, along with him to the party. The minute the music started, Thea jumped up and joined in the dancing. She danced with the same enthusiasm as the teenagers in the room did.

After the dancing died down and we were eating birthday cake, Thea came over to me, exulted. "That was so much fun—I forgot just how much I love to dance!" Then she tangoed back to George and gave him a bite of her cake and a kiss. It was clear that her Spirit was loving the party, and more important, she was loving *herself* without any reservations at all.

After the festivities were over and the house was returned to its normal appearance, I continued to think about what she'd said: "I forgot just how much I love to dance." It's true. We *do* so easily forget the things we love, the things that light up our Spirit and fill us with joy and self-love.

I know *I* do. I forget how much I cherish seeing my parents, going for bike rides with my husband, and meeting dear friends for lunch. I also fail to remember how much I love *me,* my life, and who I am when I engage in the things that are spiritually fulfilling to me.

Why is it that we're able to forget the things we love the most that make us feel good about ourselves? Why don't they seem to be priorities?

It's because we're indoctrinated to believe that it's selfish to do things simply because they make us feel happy. It's the good old American Puritan streak telling us that suffering is beneficial for the soul. I think that this is balderdash.

Seeing Thea floating away on a cloud of pure joy and squeezing George's hand in an outpouring of self-fulfilled affection, I was reminded how much connecting to what we love, and what loves *us,* is indispensable to the Spirit. It's essential to our self-love and well-being.

This was brought home to me several years ago when a woman from Omaha whom I'd never met called me to ask for a reading. She introduced herself and told me that she had stage IV breast cancer and was very near dying.

"I'm realistic, Sonia," she said. "I'm not looking for a miracle cure. I know that I don't have much longer to live. But maybe I *am* still looking for a miracle. I just want to die in peace and can't seem to find my way to it, because I forgot to live my life—the one I would have loved to live. Instead I lived "their" life—the life those around me approved of.

"I was exemplary in every way: I was a top Girl Scout. I was a model wife, PTA member, and soccer mom. I was block-party rep and a wonderful grandmother and neighbor. You name it—whatever brought me approval from others, I did it. And they did, and do, all approve of me. It's just that *I* don't approve of me. In fact, I can hardly stand myself because I feel like such a fraud. I never got around to doing what I wanted to do, what I loved, like going to Rome, or trying oil painting, or biking across Iowa.

"I missed my life by pleasing others, and now it's too late! I can't even get out of bed now. What can I possibly do now so I can die in peace? Can you tell me?"

Whoa! Her breaking heart and tragic words hit me hard. I was quiet and prayed. Then I asked my higher self and heavenly helpers for direction. *How can this woman find self-love at this stage of the game?* I wondered. *What must she know . . . what must we all know?*

In a moment the answer came through. I was guided to tell her to express her Spirit out loud and devote her remaining time and energy only to conversations about what she loved.

"Every day," I said, "tell those around you what you love. Tell them what brings you happiness, what you enjoy, the foods you like to eat, which perfumes are your favorite, what flowers touch your heart, and what movies make you happy. Tell them about everything that gives your Spirit pleasure. In doing so, you'll come back to your authentic self and find the peace and love for *you*. You'll find what you're looking for."

She was silent, and I could tell that she was thinking about what I'd just said. "That I can do," she finally answered. "In fact, I'd *love* to do that." And then she let out what sounded to me like a sigh of relief and hung up.

After this call, I realized that speaking to her was my gift for the day. She made me aware of how much I still did for the sake of approval and how much I gave priority to things that made others happy over what *I* truly loved to do. I realized how easy it was to let seeking approval become so routine that I could actually ignore what I loved and end up in the same boat as she was in.

Taking the gift from her, I decided to start attending to my Spirit more, even with the craziness of my life, and begin to at least talk about what I love more often as well. My good advice for her was good advice for *me*, too.

I invited my family and friends to join me in centering our dinner conversations around what we—all of us—loved. Happily, everyone liked the idea, and so a new tradition was founded. We started sharing our love of travel, shopping, bike trips, family gatherings, boats, movies, nature, jokes, people, Patrick's cooking, special occasions, and whatever else our collective Spirit loved.

The first thing I noticed from our experiment was how satisfying and fulfilling our dinners became. I looked forward to them and made certain that I was there. The next thing I observed was how much love I felt for myself at the end of the meal. I left the table feeling full, not just with dinner, but with my own joyful Spirit. It showed me how simply acknowledging what I love feeds and fills me with a sense of self-love!

Another thing I noticed was how this tradition subtly shifted direction from speaking about what we loved in general to what we loved that day. Even more exciting was how our behavior started changing as well. More and more we were following our Spirit toward what we loved, and our days began to be different.

For example, my daughter Sonia adores singing. Soon after our "lovefest" tradition got under way, she could be heard belting out her favorite songs at the top of her lungs throughout the house all the time, something she hadn't done before.

Patrick, who loves to cook, subtly shifted from considering making dinner a chore to putting more thought and creativity into our meals, whipping up some masterpieces and actually looking forward to serving us his latest creation.

Sabrina, who loves fashion and design, began experimenting with her outfits, showing up for dinner in more and more elaborate ensembles and really turning heads (well, *ours*, at least).

Even I shifted. I love rock and roll, the '80s, and dance parties. Soon after the new tradition began, I introduced these things to my workshops and in no time had the world (or at least *my* world) dancing with me. Work suddenly got a lot more fun!

This shift was subtle and simple. To love yourself—your authentic Spirit—simply remember, and announce, what you love. Talk about it often, to yourself and with others. Doing so effects a course correction, bringing you back to the real you. It feeds you. It fuels you. And it instills joy in you, which is one of the most self-loving things there is.

There are other simple ways you can reconnect with what your Spirit loves. One is to make a list of what you cherish. I often do this now before I go to bed and when I'm on a long airplane flight. I write mental lists when I'm waiting in line at the grocery store or post office. I even got a special notebook and designated it as my "What I Love" book.

You can take this effort a step further: Get a small tape recorder and make recordings of what you love. A great astrologer, Erica Trojan, once told me that nothing is more powerful for you than the sound of your own voice—I believe her. Several years ago I had a subliminal recording made with my own voice through a company called Holosync (**holosync.com**). I was feeling insecure about speaking to large audiences, so I made a recording that said: "I love speaking to large audiences." Apparently it worked because I do love speaking to large audiences now—almost as much as I love *dancing* with large audiences, which I manage to do every time I'm in front of one.

I work with a musician named Mark Welch (**www. musicbymarkwelch.com**) who, among other things, creates individualized CDs for people to focus on what

they love using their own voices. He overlays the recordings with customized music to make them more deeply
personal. Creating your own CD, or simply making a
recording of what you love using a small tape recorder,
is a fantastic way to remember what brings you joy and
correct your course to follow your authentic Spirit. Many
of my clients have found great success in reconnecting
with their Spirit by using this simple tool and listening
to it every day.

I listen to my recordings often. What I find is that
in the span of about 30 seconds, no matter what kind
of lousy mood I might be in, I instantly enter a brighter,
happier, more joyful state of being. I start feeling good in
my own skin and experience great love for myself.

The most important part of naming what you love,
whether by writing lists, making recordings, sharing
with friends and family, or all of the above, is that you
return to self. You develop the habit of remembering
your Spirit, and you stay more true to it. That's the most
loving thing you can do for yourself and for those in
your life.

By the way, the daughter of the woman dying of
cancer called me four months after her mother and
I spoke. She told me, "I don't know what you said,
but it had a miraculous effect on my mom. She completely changed, and started sharing things I never
knew about her—things I loved discovering. Although
she was very sick, she lightened up. She relaxed. She
laughed more. She seemed to stop struggling. And, to
the surprise of all of us, when she died, she was peaceful. And so were we."

Simple Practice: Laugh

Laughter is the voice of the Spirit. When you laugh, your Spirit is singing. To do so is to align with Heaven. Laughter frees you completely from all ego-mind connections and showers every cell in your body with God's light. It literally lightens you up energetically.

In Western culture, laughter isn't something we associate with being spiritual. We've been inundated with images of Christ suffering and dying on the cross, and not with the resurrected Christ ascending to new life. Misery and pain are profound, and, therefore, at a premium in our spiritual worldview. Laughter is frivolous and wasteful and often dismissed as irreverent and disrespectful.

As I write this, I recall moments as a child in Catholic school when I accidentally laughed at one of my nun teachers, only to be marched to the corner of the classroom to hang my head in shame. Of all the misdeeds one could commit in the classroom I attended, laughter was by far the worst.

In fact, Bobby, the class clown in third grade who made everyone laugh out loud, was eventually expelled from school for his antics. Now I understand that the teachers had their jobs to do, but to believe that we learn best in humorless, fear-filled surroundings is absurd. I remember Bobby's jokes and antics to this day, and they still make me laugh—however, I can't remember much of anything I learned from my humorless, angry teachers that year. Frankly, I prefer to forget.

In other cultures, humor is far more integrated into the sacred landscape as an important, even essential, element of spiritual health. We have the laughing Buddha, for example; or Hanuman, the Hindu monkey god full of tricks and delight. Quan Yin, the Eastern Divine mother, is usually depicted smiling; and the Native American tradition recognizes and appreciates the playfulness of the otter. There's even a sect of yoga called Laughter Yoga devoted exclusively to laughter as a way to Nirvana, which thankfully is catching on in the U.S. (**www. laughteryoga.org**).

Laughter is not only good for our Spirit, but it's our Spirit being good to *us*. Divine mind is joyful, happy, lighthearted mind. Laughter brings light to the heart and cells of the body, which creates healing.

There are now thousands and thousands of people worldwide who have followed the example of Norman Cousins—a prominent political journalist who cured himself of cancer many years ago by immersing himself in a steady flow of funny movies, joke books, and humorous stories—and have gotten the same results. They insist that humor cured them of countless diseases and physical and emotional ailments. So the verdict is in: Laughter heals.

To lose your sense of humor is to lose contact with your Spirit. To keep it no matter what is the greatest victory of Spirit over matter. In fact, I can't help but be struck by the brilliant sense of humor most survivors of trauma display. My own mother suffered so much loss as a young child in World War II that it would break my heart if I let it all in. War left her cut off from her entire family at the age of 12 when she was imprisoned in a POW camp; later, due to a case of rheumatic fever and a fall off a horse, she became deaf. Yet she has the most brilliant sense of humor of anyone I've ever known. It *saved* her.

When any form of drama and trauma presented itself in our family home, the jokes followed in short order. My mother's motto in life was, and remains to this day: *The situation is critical, but never serious.* Given all that she navigated in life, I believe her. It's a motto I've now adopted as my own.

To adopt a policy of laughter in life takes some practice and discipline. After all, as I said, it's not something that society will naturally encourage you to do. Just like any other, your laughing muscles need a regular workout. So it's best to be proactive when it comes to having as strong a sense of humor as possible.

Start by laughing at yourself. By that I mean at your overly serious, thin-skinned, self-important ego. Step back and observe its desperate attempts to try to control the world and its obvious effort to recruit others to join its cause. Notice the various antics and maneuvers your ego uses as it presses its agenda forward. One that mine uses, for example, is to get loud and indignant. My daughter Sonia's ego maneuver is to get flustered and dramatic and walk out. Patrick becomes stoic and suffers in silence. Sabrina goes ballistic, scaring us all into submission.

We each have our own way of using drama, theater, posturing, manipulation, and suffering to get life to do what we want—or at least to try to. If you take a step back and observe these antics from the perspective of Divine mind, you must admit that they're quite funny. Have a good laugh—it clears the vibration and lightens the mood with love.

If you can't laugh at yourself, you don't stand a chance of being in Divine mind. Rather, you're a complete hostage to your ego, and you can only expect misery because that's all it's capable of creating. And although everything may feel serious to you, you can be assured that those not absorbed in the drama will see you as ridiculous. So it's best to start seeing *your ego* as ridiculous first.

When I suggest laughing at yourself, I don't mean in a mean-spirited, unkind way. I just mean that you should be objective. Rise above your emotional, ego-invested suffering and see it from the outside.

The best way to laugh at yourself is to be the first to reveal your own vulnerabilities. "Tell" on yourself often. Be the first to share your floundering, embarrassments, tragedies, disappointments, and ill-fated maneuverings with others; and don't allow your ego to hide behind the fear of not being perfect.

The more painful the experience you've had, the more urgent the need to laugh about it. One of my mentors once said, "Laughter sends the devil running," meaning the world of false appearances and ego-mind illusions. Laughter instantly frees you from the grip of fear, among other things, and that alone is Heaven on Earth.

Besides, laughter bring blessings. It's contagious and brings out the Divine in everyone. Thirty years ago I set off on an adventure to France with a girlfriend. Arriving in Marseilles at midnight, with no idea where to go, we accidentally wandered into an unsavory section of town and happened upon a street brawl. Terrified, we screamed and ran, only to find ourselves confronted by police moments later and thrown into the back of their paddy wagon. Shocked, frightened, and stunned, I abruptly burst out laughing, My Spirit found it all so sudden and absurd. All I could do to absorb what was happening was to laugh . . . so much so that I couldn't stop. I laughed so hard that my friend started to giggle and then the cops did, too.

Soon, we were all laughing so hysterically that no one could speak. Once the laughter subsided, the cops figured out that we were two dumb travelers and took us to the home of one of their family members to stay. It couldn't have been better orchestrated by the angels themselves . . . on second thought, it probably *was* orchestrated by the angels. The best part is, I remained friends with the cops. Through our laughter, we bonded in Spirit.

Chuckling at yourself invites others to do the same. The more willing you are to laugh, the more immediately you enter the high frequency of Spirit. Through laughter, you can even take others with you. Rather than connecting on a "frightened, controlling ego to frightened, controlling ego" level, you communicate on a *Spirit-to-Spirit* level. Ego to ego is an unsafe place—it's a "me against you" place. Spirit to Spirit is safe because in Divine mind, we're all one. So as you laugh, not only do you *heal*, but you become the *healer* as well.

To develop your "laugh" muscles, it helps to build a library of amusing resources to draw from when life gets you down. Your laugh library can include funny movies, TV shows, and books; irreverent comics, newspapers, and comic books; amusing Internet sites; and humorous greeting cards. Start by making a list of your top 10 to 20 all-time-favorite comedy movies, and refer to it when you need a good laugh. If possible, buy the DVDs so you can just grab one and pop it in.

Some of my favorite comedic films are *This Is Spinal Tap, Best in Show, Waiting for Guffman, A Mighty Wind,*

Blades of Glory, Elf, Starsky & Hutch, The 40-Year-Old Virgin, Cat Ballou, Dick, and *Moonstruck.* These ones are just off the top of my head from the past few years. I can go further back and recall more.

When ego mind has you in its grip, it won't let you think of a funny movie. That's why it's smart to have a few ready in advance. It's also a good idea to ask friends what their favorite comedies are as well, not only to build your library, but also just to encourage lighthearted conversation. This beats the habitual commiseration the ego so easily falls into.

In addition to movies, there are, of course, humorous TV shows to use as a laughter resource as well. Every country has its own version of the American *Friends, Frasier, Everybody Loves Raymond,* and *Seinfeld*—not to mention the classics such as *I Love Lucy* or my all-time favorite, *The Jackie Gleason Show.* I end every night watching a funny rerun, and I always try to go to bed laughing.

Having copies of good TV shows or renting them from the local or online movie store is a quick way to reach for laughter when life doesn't seem very funny. The easier you make it to distract your ego with laughter, the better trained your laugh muscles will get.

The key is to choose laughter over misery. Rather than wallowing in fear or self-pity, make a Spirited choice that in the midst of life's darker moments, you'll go for the humor . . . *first.*

If you find yourself deeply stuck in ego mind, make a deal with your ego to suffer only for a while, then get to humor. For example, if you've had a bad day or have received difficult news, allow yourself 30 minutes of genuine upset. Then agree to 30 minutes of humor afterward for balance.

It will take serious discipline to adhere to this formula because, naturally, your ego won't feel like laughing —not only that, but those around you may very likely encourage your suffering. You may even be accused of using humor to escape reality.

If this is so, admit it! *Of course* you're using humor to escape the grip of the controlling, defensive, self-absorbed, humorless, and miserable ego mind. Why wouldn't you want to break free of it? In fact, thank goodness you *can* escape through laughter—that's what our Creator created it for.

We need to escape life's dramas in a healthy way from time to time, and laughter is how to do it. So be prepared, both with tools of laughter and the discipline to overcome resistance from within and without. Just announce to yourself and others that laughter is an important spiritual practice for you. Work to acquire a preference for comedy over drama. Don't be a misery addict. Download comedy skits on your iPod, and bookmark funny Websites on your computer such as **www. jokes.com**.

Put amusing screen savers on your computer. Carry comics in your wallet. Post silly sayings around the house, in the car, or in your work area. Read humorous books—of course, I don't mean exclusively, but do have a healthy inflow of good lighthearted laugh material to balance the weight of the world.

Practice making light of life. Humor and wit exercise the brain. Laugh out loud, often, even if you don't feel like it. Forced laughter eventually leads to the real thing. And fake laughter is better than none at all. Besides, it makes you aware of just how much your ego has you in its grip and won't let you find humor. If you fake laughter, your Spirit is at least in the process of breaking free.

I recently watched an episode of *Oprah* on the subject of happiness. On this particular show, Oprah's makeup artist came on the program and expressed how miserable he was over a significant relationship breakup and how he couldn't stop crying.

He then attended a "laugh-fest," a group where people laugh for the sake of it. He started out resistant, judgmental, uncooperative, and not invested in lightening up at all. His ego mind was hardly in the mood to be happy, and these forced laughers annoyed the heck out of him.

Nevertheless, he joined in and halfheartedly went through the motions—only to his surprise, he caught the Spirit of the gathering and in less than 15 minutes, he genuinely started to have fun and laugh for real. Like all manifestations of Spirit, the laughter of others was contagious. Soon, it was too difficult to remain miserable in the collective vibration of joy. He threw his despair to the wind and started to laugh and join the others with gusto.

When it was over, he'd forgotten his woes. He felt great, which surprised him. He actually had to make an effort to find his misery once again. He did, but he had to look for it.

Laughing is Spirit taking charge of your life. It's freedom from the ego. It's Divine-mind perspective and absolutely the best medicine you have.

To laugh *at* life, *with* life, *in* life, *about* life is to live your Spirit fully. It's one of the most soul-affirming acts of self-love you can choose. Practice laughing out loud just for the sake of it. Remember how as children you and your friends often tried to make each other crack up by laughing in a silly way? It worked then—it will work now.

❁ ❁ ❁

STEP 8

Accept Life's Lessons with Grace

Simple Lesson: Accept Life's Lessons with Grace

This step erases the illusion that self-love and joy in life are only possible when problems go away. The practice that follows clears the thick, heavy fog of emotional fear and anxiety. You'll stop trying to earn affection and start feeling the unconditional love that your Spirit and God have for you, now and always.

❀

Perhaps the biggest obstacle to loving yourself and living your Spirit is the belief that you can only do so when all your problems are solved, all your worries are alleviated, and all your concerns and fears have disappeared. The truth is, this will never happen. As long as you're in a physical body and possess a human ego, you must live with the stuff of being human.

We're not here to get over our humanness, but rather to accept and make peace with it. And yet we mustn't allow our human experiences to distract us from living the peace and personal joy of our Divine self and our Spirit. Being human brings challenges—that goes with the territory. Not all of them are the same, yet we all have an equal share. In fact, facing our challenges with good Spirit is the primary sport of the human experiment. As souls, we incarnate to learn certain lessons, the most important of these being to remember our Divine nature while having human experiences.

Life's lessons, challenges, concerns, obstacles, recurring themes, and difficult patterns make up what we colloquially call the "stuff" of our lives. Every one of us—from the beggar in India to the broker on Wall Street to the Dalai Lama—has "stuff" or personal soul work that provides challenges. Even Mother Teresa, who is revered as a modern-day saint, struggled with a lot of "stuff" in her life. Recently, in fact, a collection of her personal letters revealed how she even doubted her faith in God.

These lessons, or the "stuff" of our lives, are our souls' work. They may be lessons of love, of creating prosperity, or of physical health. They may be ones of trust and commitment or of relationships and family. They may be lessons of poverty, abandonment, and loss . . . or just the opposite—of wealth, acquisition, and devotion.

No matter the lessons we encounter in life, there are several things of which we may be certain:

1. First, we can know that on a soul level, we volunteered to learn the lessons facing us, whatever they are.

2. Second, there's no lesson we run across that's too difficult for our soul to learn.

3. And finally, once we learn a soul lesson,
    another will take its place. Lessons will never
    stop presenting themselves as long as we're
    alive.

The very reason we've taken on a physical reality is to grow our soul, which we do through facing challenges. Life is school for the soul and, therefore, should be embraced—difficult lessons and all. Unlike human school, where we graduate and then are expected to enter the "real world," when it comes to the soul, the "real" world is that of endless lessons, one after another, encountered throughout our entire physical existence as a means to reclaim our Divinity.

It's not getting beyond our "stuff," overcoming our personal challenges, rising above our doubts, and conquering difficult situations that gives us the permission to love ourselves and live our Spirit—quite the opposite. It's rather the ability to love ourselves and live our Spirit that gives us the means by which we can face and successfully work through our stuff and learn our lessons.

We all have soul work; we all have areas of personal growth and spiritual maturity to develop. Don't let your lessons rob you of your joy. Instead, cultivate joy of the Spirit to help you successfully work through life's stuff. If you deprive yourself of love and kindness, you'll fail to learn anything. You must love your Spirit and listen to it, because without doing so, you won't be able to honestly or capably overcome any challenges. Only self-love and faithful expression of your Spirit teach you what you must learn.

Don't allow your ego to convince you that your stuff is more serious than it is, or more profound or important than the next person's, thereby giving you permission to wallow in it.

Mother Teresa dealt with the poorest and sickest of India under the worst of conditions and still managed to love herself and live her Spirit. The Dalai Lama lost his entire country yet must serve as the spiritual light for hundreds of thousands of displaced souls—this is very difficult stuff. However, he is filled with absolute joy.

Your present-day challenge may feel no less difficult right now. That it is so is exactly the reason to love yourself and live your Spirit—so you can work through it. It's far better to approach any problem with the love of Spirit rather than the fear and control of the ego.

Living your Spirit allows you to see beyond life's immediate drama and points you toward solutions. Self-love helps you access your creativity and solve problems. It reduces conflict and eases fear. Your Spirit is your best ally when facing pain of any sort. It gets you past, through, or over your "stuff" more quickly.

For example, my client Marion had a son in prison for sexually abusing his own 12-year-old daughter and had another son living on the street with a heroin addiction. She'd also been diagnosed with early-stage colon cancer. By any standards, hers was quite a bit of "stuff."

For the first six months after her son went to prison and she received the cancer diagnosis, Marion languished in shame and fear, becoming more and more depressed—and sicker as well. One night, at the end of her rope, she went to bed and prayed for a miracle. The next morning she woke up and found herself suddenly feeling a bit stronger than she had felt in months, if not years. Not exactly sure why she felt better, she didn't question it. She simply rejoiced.

Suddenly, around noon it occurred to her what exactly was different: She wasn't beating herself up about all the problems she faced anymore. Somehow her prayers had been miraculously answered in the night. She was free of the inner tyranny that her ego had relentlessly subjected her to. There was no more blaming and shaming for everything that wasn't going well in her life. In its place was a peaceful acceptance that the issues at hand were simply her lot to face in life and nothing more. In her sudden clarity, she knew that she would get through.

The first change was that she stopped agonizing over her sons. Instead, she put her efforts into getting better. With determination and focus—and God's grace—she recovered from the cancer. Next, she adopted her granddaughter. Not able to undo what had happened, she knew that she could at least help her granddaughter not blame herself. She was also aware that she couldn't teach the girl to love herself if she, Marion, didn't do the same. So she accepted the challenge and began to self-love in earnest. She spoke kindly to herself. She ate well. She went to bed early. She appreciated her strength. And she forgave the past.

Not only did she recover her health, but she also recovered her heart. The gift behind all of this tragedy was that in addition to learning to self-love, she also received the beautiful gift of guardianship of her granddaughter . . . and the most delightful love she'd ever known.

She even understood why her sons had such difficulties. They didn't have self-love, either, which drove them to such heinous behaviors. Marion forgave them and even began to send them love, something not possible before. I don't know what happened to her sons. I *do* know that Marion and her granddaughter moved to another state and started a small lavender farm together and are now living in healthy, quiet peace.

❋

The best way to remain self-loving and aligned with Spirit when facing life's challenges is to remember that they all are lessons—so stop feeling as though you're a victim. This isn't to suggest that the ones you face at times aren't difficult or painful. It only means that until you acknowledge that your challenges exist to teach you something on a soul level, you can't even begin to get past or rise above them. Whatever problem you encounter, know that it presents itself because there's something in that situation that your soul wants to learn. The more quickly you acknowledge your problems as opportunities to acquire wisdom, the more manageable they become.

For example, in my life, my primary "stuff" or soul lessons have centered on my partnership with my husband. On a personality level, he and I are like oil and water. Consequently, we don't see or experience life in the same way, and this has led to conflict over the years.

If I let my ego deal with the situation, I could suffer tremendously over our differences and not allow myself to feel love or my Spirit at all. But, fortunately, by the grace of God and a few great teachers, I don't allow my ego to run the course, at least not most of the time. I know on a soul level that intimacy and partnership are my challenges for growth, and I accept this lesson. It can be difficult upon occasion, but loving my authentic self and being good to my Spirit makes it far easier.

Self-love allows me to confront my "stuff" with my husband with greater resiliency, humor, creativity, and compassion. These gifts of my Spirit help me with my soul lesson. I'm the first to admit that I haven't yet mastered my lessons in this area, but we *have* been married 26 years and counting, and every day—with the love and help of my Spirit—it's getting easier and easier.

My friend Debra has different soul lessons to contend with in her life. Personal relationships and intimacy have come easily to her, and she's quite peaceful in her partnerships. Her "stuff" centers more on money. She has difficulty creating prosperity and feeling financially secure.

After being laid off from a job of 25 years, she has lived from paycheck to paycheck, often falling short of acquiring the means to take care of her bills. However, she does love herself and live her Spirit, so although the uncertainty of her financial future is challenging, she still enjoys a peaceful assurance that all will somehow work out. This fearless confidence, arising from her Spirit, keeps her ego from collapsing with fear.

This isn't to suggest that she doesn't have her moments, or even days, of stress. She most certainly does. But, behind these waves of anxiety lies a deeper pool of confidence that's centered in her Spirit. Her trust in Divine Source reassures her as she lives day to day. The end result is that even in the face of financial uncertainty, she's able to enjoy her life—and does. And, miraculously, she's managing to stay financially afloat.

I have a client named Alan who, paradoxically, is in a sound financial situation yet is obsessed with worry about losing it all. As a highly disciplined self-employed man, he has managed to pay off his mortgage and car loan and save a hefty amount for retirement. Yet because he resonates with ego mind over self-love and his Divine Spirit, he's consumed with fear and anxiety about his security all the time, which makes him agitated and short with friends and loved ones. It caused him to lash out at his two employees, one of whom had had enough abuse from him and recently quit.

Because judgment and self-loathing have infected his consciousness, he believes that the entire financial world is on the verge of collapse. He rehearses disaster after disaster in his imagination and doesn't allow himself any reprieve. His ego affords him no time off, no vacation, and no rest for fear that if he allows himself these things, his security will be sacrificed. He's so buried in his "stuff" that he has completely lost sight of all objectivity.

Without self-love or connection to his Spirit to guide him, he's absolutely miserable. He can't feel peace in his own accomplishments. Furthermore, his negative energy infects those around him with the same unhealthy frequency, setting off a chain reaction of misery. It's not a pretty sight.

Alan isn't unique. The majority of people I work with suffer similarly. Not knowing that their challenges are simply cultivating a self-loving Spirit, people wallow and struggle in victimhood. The way out is simple: Just own your stuff. In other words, acknowledge your challenges and understand that they're not personal assaults on your worth (even though they do feel like it at times), but rather lessons your soul simply wants to learn, and can.

For example, I want to learn how to create intimacy without getting swallowed up by my partner. Debra wants to learn to use her wealth of talents to manifest material wealth. Alan wants to learn self-worth. So far, he's not learning very quickly, but eventually he will—as soon as he stops relying on his self-loathing, fearful ego to guide him. It's only when he starts loving and following his Spirit that he'll find peace.

In what areas do *you* feel victimized? Wherein lies *your* frustration? Pain? Challenge? Irritation? Annoyance? Struggle? Loss? Where those are, so are your soul lessons.

Next, ask yourself if your ego is taking a beating or if it's beating up your Spirit over these lessons by being judgmental, impatient, critical, wounded, angry, embarrassed, indignant, fearful, or disgusted. If the latter is so, you've fallen out of integrity and alignment with your Spirit and have disconnected from self-love.

Negative energies only further deepen or complicate your problems and prevent you from learning. Step back and view any problem as a soul lesson—not personal penance or punishment—just a class, like any other. The only way to successfully "pass" it is with detached self-love and connection to your Spirit.

If we look at our stuff from the perspective of the ego, we take it quite personally. We get overwhelmed, demoralized, weakened, and fearful. If we choose to view our challenges and lessons from self-love and Spirit, we see them as the game and sport they're intended to be. This doesn't mean we won't feel pain—pain goes with the human experience. Rather, it just reminds us that our Spirit is greater than any hurt the ego or body will ever feel.

The only way to meet life's problems head-on and overcome them successfully with peace in your heart is to approach them in Spirit. Filled with self-love, you'll discover that the sweet love your Creator has for you will ease your way, remove obstacles more quickly, and help you navigate everything on the human plane with grace. The greater the problem, the more critical it is to love yourself. Problems aren't your fault. They just *are*. And solutions can always be found through love.

Simple Practice: Keep Moving

Your Spirit is an active, powerful energy—it's a dancing flame, a rushing wind, a crashing wave of holiness. Your ego has no life force—it's a robotic machine churning over and over the same fearful, controlling, negative patterns and messages. They each have distinctly different vibrations: One is alive and engages with life; the other is empty and drains it.

When you're aligned and resonating with your gorgeous Spirit, every cell in your body is energized. When you resonate with your ego, your body often comes to a paralyzed standstill. It becomes locked in negative patterns much the way a computer with a virus gets frozen and seizes up.

One of the best ways to prevent yourself from getting "seized up" by the ego and its debilitating frequency is to consciously align with life and use the life force of your Spirit to move. When you do so, you engage your Spirit. Have you ever heard the expression "The Spirit moved me"? When your Spirit is embodied, it *does* move you, and in a way that's far more profound and graceful than the movement that comes from struggling with the ego.

I was just watching the popular television show *America's Next Top Model.* On the program, 12 gorgeous girls all compete for the honor of being named America's next top model by going through a series of challenges to capture a great photo. The show I happened upon was one where the models had to dance while being photographed.

Here's where it got interesting: Although they all moved *to* the music, only some of them were moved *by* it and truly danced. By that I mean it was visually obvious which girls were going through loveless, spiritless, fearful, controlled motions and which ones were surrendering to their inner rhythm. It was difficult to watch the models who were controlled by their fearful egos; at the same time, it was thrilling to watch those who fully surrendered their Spirit to the dance.

On strictly a skill level, all their movements were equal. They were all flopping and bopping in much the same way. It was the energy and essence of their movements, rather, that made the difference. The ones who let go were beautiful and inspiring to behold; the ones who didn't were awkward and painful to watch.

At first I wondered if I was being overly discerning, as I'm so tuned in to Spirit. Apparently not. The judges had exactly the same reaction I did. The girls who let their Spirit go were advanced to the next level. The ones who didn't were eliminated.

All right, I can hear the objection: Not every person is a dancer, right? Except the truth is, everybody *is* one at heart. The human Spirit expresses itself best in dance. Only the ego blocks the dance of Spirit, something that's painful to see and even more so to live.

In fact, one of the best, most direct, immediately self-affirming Spirit-loving activities you can ever engage in is dance. And by that I mean move with commitment to the rhythm. Turn on some great music that speaks to your Spirit and go for it—you'll see what I mean. Like laughing, dancing catches you by surprise and pulls you in if you do it long enough.

Even if you initially don't have the urge to dance, give it a few minutes and see what happens. Often the ego surrenders after five to ten minutes, and your Spirit can then step in. Your ego will still try to get you to stop, but it only has so much energy for resistance and then it usually gives up. Once it stops resisting, you soar to a higher vibration. Dancing completely expresses your Spirit and invigorates your vibration with pure joy.

Recently I was teaching this lesson in the U.K. when an indignant woman raised her hand with an objection. "What if you're handicapped?" she asked, with "gotcha" gusto. To this I shared the story of Jennifer, my client who walks with crutches—and with great difficulty at that. Not to be deprived of her dance, she has put long colorful ribbons on her crutches and lets them sway to the music with her as a way to dance.

Another client, Mary, who was born without legs and only partial arms, bounces up and down and sways side to side in her wheelchair. She cites dancing as one of her most physically and soulfully liberating outlets. She loves it, and it's obvious.

So to such objections I answer that dancing is an attitude more than an aptitude. It allows your Spirit to step forward and take over. If you want to dance, you can.

Years ago I attended a lecture here in Chicago given by a well-known anthropologist named Jean Houston, who sang the praises of dancing as being essential for the Spirit. She shared a story I'll never forget. She said that there was a little-known tribe in Africa who had virtually no history of conflict. When the group was studied to see how they resolved difficulties, it was discovered that whenever there was an argument or issue among members, the entire tribe went to the center of the village and danced until everybody was over the problem. What a marvelous idea!

Can you imagine if world leaders were asked to dance with each other until they surrendered to the movement, and only then could they negotiate? I'm certain we'd have very different results on a global level.

Dance isn't the only way to live your Spirit through movement, however. Something as simple as taking a brisk walk for as little as 15 minutes is also an effective antidote for an attack of ego in order to get back to your Spirit. It's a fail-safe, self-loving method for leaving the energy of ego mind behind and moving to the peace and tranquility of Divine mind.

For the energetic, taking the walk up to a run works wonders as well. The minute you run, your ego has to give up control because it's your Spirit that advances you. All runners I know call it a spiritual experience. I call running (and walking and dancing) a "Spirited" experience.

Whether it's walking, swimming, running, dancing, skiing, biking, Rollerblading, skipping, or any other method of movement that calls you, my point is to love yourself and live your Spirit through physical activity every day. Committed movement calms the ego, clears the brain fog, quiets the chatter, and leads you to the frequency and vibration of Divine mind. It's hard for the ego to rant, rave, and ruminate while your blood is pumping and your heart rate is up. The body serves the

Spirit, not the ego. When you move, you engage your physical self as your ally.

I once read that if a person who was abused or victimized gets caught up in a flashback, the first thing they must do is stand up and start moving quickly. They can pace back and forth, jump up and down—anything. This unfreezes the negative loop of past memories and brings the person back to the present time and a higher vibration. Since we've all been abused or victimized at some point (or at least our egos believe that we have), this is a powerful tool of self-love and Spirit expression that we can all use.

Part of the reason why I believe people have gotten so far away from movement and from being comfortable in their bodies is because our education system calls such activity "extracurricular," something not essential to our learning process. Children are still deprived of movement and recess if they misbehave. Instead of being allowed to go outside and shake things out a bit and call their Spirit home, they're put in corners, forced to sit and stew in bad vibes. It's so utterly wrong.

We got—and still get—the message that movement is an unnecessary indulgence rather than a basic tool of self-love and of living our Spirit. It's time to cast that oppressive message off. Movement in whatever form calls us should be part of our spiritual practice. It's essential to keeping our Spirit embodied and present.

You don't have to sweat to get the self-loving benefit of moving. It's optional, even recommended, but to some a good game of golf or a stroll through the arboretum is as soul satisfying as jumping on a trampoline. In fact, the best way to confirm that a movement is engaging your Spirit is to notice your vibration before, during, and after your activity. If you feel grounded, peaceful, and calm in your heart and "in" present time, your movement has served you well.

Movement is certainly one of the first tools to reach for when your ego mind is manipulating you into self-doubt. The more quickly you move, the more quickly you ditch the ego and free yourself to get back home.

In addition to simply moving, you can take the power of this tool to self-love even higher by going out of doors when you move. Outside is Earth, your Divine mother who delights in you. She gives you beautiful gifts that you can only notice if you do go outside, such as trees, flowers, sky, birds, squirrels, beaches, mountains, and valleys.

Just this summer my ego mind had seized up on me and was causing a hearty round of rather disruptive anxiety about how I would ever find the time to write with my travel schedule laid out as it was. Fed up with the distraction, I marched outside and over to Lincoln Park, near my home. As I walked, I became mesmerized with all I saw: barbecues hosted by people of every nationality in the world, volleyball games, drumming circles, and soccer matches, all against the backdrop of a crystal blue sky and an azure Lake Michigan. The city was at its best and nature was, too.

Continuing my stroll, I happened upon a bird sanctuary that I knew was there but somehow had never visited. It was teeming with gorgeous birds of all sizes and colors, and butterflies as well. I was absolutely captivated by the beauty. I only walked for an hour all told yet felt as if I had traveled around the world. The best part of my walk outdoors was how, shortly into it, I completely forgot my worries. Even my ego was enthralled with the marvel of the outdoors. It gave me perspective and I stopped worrying, and that was that.

Going outside and moving with nature are wonderful ways to love yourself and live your Spirit. Nature feeds your Spirit. Venture outdoors and notice the scenery right now and observe how you feel afterward. Are you in ego mind or Divine mind? See what I mean?

Taking the idea of movement to another level, a simple way to love yourself and live your Spirit is to change the scenery. Doing so is like switching the channel from ego mind to Divine mind. When you intentionally change the scenery to get a break from the disruptions and upset of ego mind, you affirm your right as Divine Spirit to live in peace. It's a proactive way to choose peace.

I've experienced the power of changing the scenery firsthand many times over. Years ago my husband, Patrick, and I—at the time the parents of two young children and in the midst of renovating an old Victorian home — often found ourselves overextended and overwhelmed. As a result, we started snapping at, nagging, and fighting with each other out of fear, because we both felt so out of control of our situation, and it made our egos miserable.

Every time it got particularly tense at home, we hopped into our car and took a drive into Wisconsin, about 100 miles north of Chicago. For the first 50 miles or so we wouldn't even speak to one another. During the final 50, however, we'd begin to chat about the scenery. Then we'd turn around and head back, agreeing to talk about anything but our problems. We made a policy *not* to discuss our conflicts and only to enjoy the drive. By the time we returned, our troubles felt less serious and we could look at them more objectively. Changing the scenery gave us perspective and helped distract us from our fear. Those drives got us through the most difficult years of our married life together.

Changing the scenery is actually an age-old wisdom. It's called "vacation." A vacation gives the ego and all of its concerns a rest and feeds the Spirit with adventure, nature, relaxation, recreation, different foods, new people, and most of all, a huge dose of being in the present.

When you enter the unfamiliar or out of the ordinary, your ego doesn't have the luxury of droning on and on about past and future concerns and fears. It has to pay attention to the now. The ego mind lives in the past and future. The Spirit, however, resides only in the present. So when you're required to pay attention, you're in the now. When your Spirit takes over, your vibration elevates, and the peace and quiet of Divine mind kicks in.

※ ※ ※

STEP 9

Engage Music

Simple Lesson: Engage Music

This step gives you direct access to your heavenly resources and immediately lightens your heart through music. It shows you how to consciously engage music as an antidote to the negativity of the world and use it to keep your Spirit strong and resilient no matter what occurs around you. The practice that follows aims to have you choose celebration and joy as a daily experience rather than hoping it happens <u>to</u> you. You'll start to experience life as a gift and waste no time in enjoying it fully.

❁

Music is vibratory fuel. The Spirit is a vibratory body; and music steadies, reinforces, and grounds it in our denser physical vehicles and keeps it happy.

When we hear music that resonates with our Spirit, we immediately shift away from fear and reconnect with our timeless Divine nature. Music moves the body and connects us to the flow. When we hear it, we momentarily take a break from thinking and simply feel. It clears negativity, brings us into the present, and opens our heart.

When connecting to music that speaks to our heart, we relax into the vibratory frequency of trust. Music rejuvenates us on a cellular level. To connect with the particular variety that moves our soul is one of the easiest self-loving choices we can make. Music is the language of Spirit, and it brings release from all that bogs our lives down.

Listen to beautiful music every day—it will strengthen your inner light. The key is to do so without interruption. Tuning in to the radio, with fast-talking DJs and commercials, doesn't create nearly the same level of inner brilliance as does listening to music without breaks.

Be certain to listen at a volume that moves your Spirit but doesn't assault your body. It's self-defeating, for example, to play "Stairway to Heaven" while destroying your eardrums. That's not self-loving. You want your ears to enjoy what you're listening to and not feel bombarded by it.

I have a friend named Elizabeth who found clarity and solace in music after experiencing an extremely tumultuous year. Her husband all but abandoned her by relocating his business to another city without discussing it with her first. To add insult to injury, she discovered by accident that to finance his new venture, he'd mortgaged their house for over a million dollars and started a partnership with a man who was in federal prison.

Prior to discovering all of this, she'd made plans to go to Telluride, Colorado, with her husband to see the summer bluegrass festival. Her friends and family immediately suggested that she cancel her plans. How on earth, they argued, could she possibly go on a vacation with someone who had so blatantly violated her confidence? Furthermore, how could she justify the expense, given that she just found out she was now partner to an outrageous debt?

These were legitimate arguments for calling off the trip, or so her ego said. But her Spirit rebelled. To call off the trip would feed her fears, indulge her victimhood, and put her in a place to feel like a martyr. But it would do nothing positive for her Spirit. Quite the opposite—it would deny her Spirit a great source of joy.

Elizabeth wouldn't succumb. The trip was already paid for, and going wouldn't hurt anyone. Yes, she felt betrayed by her husband for his self-serving business practices and sneaky refinancing, and she was angry. But at the same time she realized that to call off the trip to spite him would only further hurt *her*. The same was true of going alone: She wanted to share the experience of mountain biking, camping, and enjoying the music with him, not experience them by herself. Those things fed her Spirit.

So she kept her plans intact, and off they went, although she was by no means at peace about it . . . that is, until the music started. Standing in front of center stage, she heard the very first strum of the very first banjo and at that moment all the negativity and anxiety that surrounded her flowed out of her bones, out of her body, out of her aura, and finally out of her being altogether.

The music, the vibratory food for her Spirit, was transmitting real energy and life force to her. The more she listened, the higher her vibration became. She danced, she sang, and she lost herself in the ecstasy of the music. Nothing else mattered. This went on for several days.

She intuitively knew without question that her husband's struggle to be creative took him to the other city, where he was able to avail himself of more opportunities than where they lived. She also knew that in no way had he intended to deceive her about his financing and partnering decisions. Rather, he had meant to protect her—he wanted to keep her from worry. She also knew, after a particularly rewarding jam session with a beloved band at the festival, that although seemingly dubious, her husband's projects were sound and would work out. She was absolutely financially safe and secure.

The most important part of this story is that none of these profound and accurate revelations came about from a dialogue between the two of them. She simply "got it," slipping out of the vibration of subjective ego-based fear and into the flow of her Divine self through the conduit of the music. The bluegrass festival fed her Spirit, rejuvenated her cells, shifted her vibration, and gave her access to her authentic self. From there she knew with certainty beyond words that both her Spirit and earthly worlds, in spite of appearances, weren't going to collapse.

❁

I've had so many experiences where music led me back to my authentic self when many other avenues failed. Listening to David Bowie brought me to my first breakthrough experience in manifestation. I played his *Ziggy Stardust and the Spiders from Mars* album daily while imagining attracting a boyfriend—one who liked to dance and was as outrageous as I was. I met Randy three weeks later. I knew that he was a keeper because he wore red rhinestone platform shoes that matched my white rhinestone platform shoes. We were an item throughout high school.

In addition, listening to Led Zeppelin's "Going to California" gave me the resolve to study abroad, Gregorian chants opened me up to writing, and Beethoven's Ninth Symphony lent me the courage to teach.

I'm not alone in being fed by music. It feeds every soul. My friend Louise swears that having Mozart playing in the background in the hospital cured her of Hodgkin's disease. Even Einstein attributes the stimulus for his theory of relativity to music.

Bob Dylan is my daughter Sabrina's soul food. Pink Floyd is the main ingredient for my other daughter's musical feast. Mozart speaks to my husband. I like good old rock and roll.

Consciously connect to music as one of your non-negotiable sources of self-love. It's powerful fuel for your Spirit. When you disconnect from it, you disconnect from your Spirit. And when you gain access to your authentic self (which can only be done through acts of self-love), you can see the Big Picture, going beyond your fears and to the truth. Only then can you make the highest, most informed choices for your well-being.

Simple Practice: Celebrate Life

The way to wholeness, satisfaction, and tremendous inner peace is to live from your Spirit and celebrate it. To celebrate life is to enjoy it—to engage in it without guilt, fear, or control and instead accept and embrace it for the grand adventure that it is.

To enjoy life is easy. Start by simply noticing it around you. You can begin in your own kitchen as you eat breakfast. Notice the fragrant smell of the coffee as it brews. Observe the beautiful color of your orange juice as you pour it into a glass. Pay attention to the "snap, crackle, pop" of your Rice Krispies as you pour milk over them. If you notice life right in front of your face, it's very entertaining to the senses.

Look around your environment and notice something you've overlooked or have never fully seen or experienced before, such as the detailing in the fabric on your furniture or the intricate white patterns on the orchid leaves in your living room.

We have delightful creations all around us, yet if we're mesmerized by our ego mind, we don't even pay attention to them—that is, until they aren't there anymore. Only then do we recognize the joy they brought us.

I was reminded of this several years ago when we had a goldfish that swam 'round and 'round in a fish tank on our kitchen counter. He had an unusually shaped head, so we named him Brainy. Brainy lived for years and years. Someone fed him once a day, but other than that we rarely stopped to notice him one way or the other.

One afternoon as I was standing with my husband next to the fish tank, I looked in and noticed that Brainy was gone. Puzzled, I asked Patrick if he knew where Brainy was. Looking into the tank, he, too, was surprised and quite confused. Immediately our suspicions turned to a new housekeeper we'd hired several days earlier.

"Oh no! Do you think the housekeeper killed and flushed Brainy?" I wondered.

Thinking the worst and upset at the thought, Patrick indignantly said, "Maybe, but that's pretty bold if she did." Peering into the empty tank, he added, "That makes me angry!"

Not believing someone would actually ditch the family pet, even if it was only a goldfish, Patrick reached into the aquarium to see if Brainy was hiding behind something and we just didn't see him. It was a fruitless effort, because the only thing in the tank was an old conch shell in the corner.

As he moved the shell, our daughters walked in from playing soccer. "What are you doing?" they asked, seeing us both hovering over the aquarium.

"Looking for Brainy," I said. "Have you seen him?"

"No!" they shrieked, upset to hear that Brainy was missing. "Where is he? Oh my God, what's happened to Brainy? Did he die?"

"I don't know," replied Patrick, puzzled. "He's just gone." Just to be certain, Patrick pulled out the conch shell so as not to miss anything, but as he did, he heard something flopping around inside the shell. He shook it a few times and sure enough, a *flop, flop, flop* was audible.

"I think he's trapped inside the shell," Patrick said.

"Shake it again," I urged. Sure enough, we could all hear *flop, flop, flop.*

"Oh my gosh—he's inside!" I screamed, going into emergency mode. "Shake him out. He'll die without water."

Patrick kicked into 911 action. He shook and shook the shell, but Brainy didn't fall out. By now the girls were screaming, too, fearing for the goldfish's life. "Hurry, Dad! He'll die if you don't hurry." Shake as he might, all he could do was flop Brainy around inside.

"We have to break the shell open," Patrick said. "He's stuck."

By now Brainy had been without water for at least a minute. Time was of the essence. "Hurry!" we screamed. "Break it!"

Patrick rushed out the back door and slammed the shell on the sidewalk, trying to break it. It didn't work, so he smashed it again and again. My daughters and I hysterically urged him on. "Harder, smash it harder. Hurryyy! He'll die!"

The fourth attempt worked: The conch shell broke open and Brainy flew out. We screamed as Patrick caught him in midair with both hands. By now at least five minutes had passed since Brainy had been in the water. We rushed back to the aquarium, Patrick leading the way, and threw the fish in. No doubt traumatized by lack of water, aggressive shaking, and ultimately being slammed into the sidewalk, Brainy lay there motionless, floating on the water.

"He's dead!" the girls moaned in despair. "Brainy's dead!" They burst into tears. Holding hands and crying, we all stared in shock at the goldfish's motionless body.

Ten seconds later, Brainy jerked and then jerked again. "Look!'" screamed Patrick. We couldn't believe our eyes. Brainy jerked again and then, just as though nothing had happened, took off swimming.

"Hooray!" we screamed, hugging one another with joy at Brainy's resuscitation. Staring into the aquarium, all four of us couldn't believe our luck that Brainy had survived. We were in pure bliss watching our bulbous-headed goldfish swim slowly back and forth.

Brainy taught us all something important that day: to appreciate life and take none of it for granted. Never before was I as happy to see Brainy as I was the day after his near-death experience. He lived on to give us five more years of beautiful days, because every time we saw him from that moment forward, we felt his presence as a gift not to be overlooked.

⁂

Celebrating life is an act of Spirit. It clears the mental fog and confusion of feeling sorry for yourself and reminds you to remember that everything in life is a gift. Every moment, every experience, is a gift from God for you to appreciate.

It's so easy for the ego to distract you from all there is to celebrate. It takes life's gifts for granted, shoving them aside and encouraging you to ignore them, while pining away for what's not there instead. How easy it is to forget that everything is a gift, and every gift is a reason to celebrate.

Twenty-six years ago I had an experience that has stayed with me ever since, reminding me always to celebrate life. I was preparing to get married, and as a wedding gift my sister paid to have my aunt and uncle travel from then-Communist Romania to attend the ceremony. It was the first time any of my mother's relatives would visit the States or meet her family since she had been separated from them as a child during World War II.

When they arrived, they were overwhelmed by the abundance flowing everywhere. The most poignant moment, however, was when we stopped at the local grocery store to buy dinner and took them along. When my aunt and uncle, who had been accustomed to so little, saw the shelves upon shelves of fresh food, pro-duce, meats, and fish, they were overcome with emo-tion. They could barely speak, and both of them cried. "To think there is this much to enjoy," they said, trying to take it all in.

What was to be a quick run to the store turned into a three-hour excursion as they strolled through the aisles, smelling produce, tasting the day's samples, and looking at shelf after shelf of offerings. They marveled at every-thing, and seeing it through their eyes, I did, too.

It was indeed a gift that we as Americans had such easy access to such abundance, and it was worth cele-brating. My wedding—with my aunt and uncle in atten-dance—was a truly incredible celebration of love, life, family, and appreciation. If ever I feel deprived or sorry for myself, I need only think of that day and my Spirit soars once again.

With my mom growing up during the war and my dad growing up during the Depression years, we were raised to celebrate the small things in life all the time. Because the abundance available to us wasn't something they took for granted, we were encouraged not to do so either.

Fridays in our home were a cause for great celebra-tion because it was ice-cream day. At the end of the week, my father got paid at work and always stopped by the local creamery and brought home two gallons of hand-packed ice cream, just enough to give his family of seven kids their fill. We sang folk songs at the top of our lungs as we enjoyed our bowls of ice cream together. It was a weekly party.

Another tradition my mother instituted was the "Weren't We Great Party." For this Friday-night gathering, we took turns telling each other about one of our greatest moments during the week. It could have been when one of us aced a test at school, helped a friend, made a basket on the basketball court, baked a homemade cake, or managed to finish our homework on time. The point wasn't so much to commemorate what we did as it was simply to celebrate life.

This taught us to make our own party rather than waiting to be invited to someone else's. To this day I love to enjoy a good "Weren't We Great Party" with my family and friends. It's a reason to laugh, to acknowledge ourselves and others, and to appreciate the good things in life.

You don't need an excuse to celebrate. To love yourself and all of life's abundance and blessings is reason enough. Life is a beautiful gift, and every day brings with it so much cause to celebrate that it's simply time you do. Don't wait to be invited to life's party. Be the party yourself.

Start by celebrating the little things. If you're alive, that in itself is a good reason. If you have clothes on your back, a roof over your head, and people who love you, then you have every reason in the world to celebrate. Rejoice in good days because you accomplished positive things. Celebrate difficult days because you got through them.

I had a young client named Jeremy who was diagnosed with a brain tumor at 22 years old. With a bleak prognosis and his healing options running out, he decided to celebrate his birthday every day he had left. He sang "Happy Birthday" to himself, bought himself cards, and treated himself to balloons and festivities.

Jeremy had been given three months to live; he actually lived two more *years*. Right before he died, we spoke.

He said, "The best gift I ever received was my tumor. I existed for 22 years, but I wasn't alive. After my tumor, I woke up and have enjoyed every minute as if there were no tomorrow, and I've had more fun and joy than in all the prior 22 years."

❀   ❀   ❀

STEP 10

Choose Kindness

Simple Lesson: Choose Kindness

This step strives to have you share your Spirit with those around you. In doing so, its light becomes even stronger and more powerful. The practice that follows permanently connects you to the inner guidance of your Spirit, eliminating moments of confusion and fear and replacing them with confidence. At the same time, you'll also become a catalyst for awakening the Spirit in others. This is the greatest experience of self-love and Spirit-guided living you can hope to have. No longer struggling in the dark, you become a light in the world.

The greatest joy the Spirit knows is to share its light and love with others. Unlike the ego—which is driven by the question *What's in it for me?*—the Spirit feels complete and wants to share this satisfaction with as many as possible. To share our Spirit with another is one of the most healing and empowering experiences we can create for ourselves. Happily, the way is simple: All we must do is be kind.

Kindness is our loving Spirit in action. It allows our Divine nature to take over and lead our lives. When we're kind, we embody this nature and use it to feed and fuel the light in the world.

To be kind is to live with grace, dignity, and elegance. It means taking an interest in life and caring about it enough to make it better for you and others. It's a powerful and profoundly self-loving choice, primarily because the law of the Universe dictates that what goes around comes around. In other words, every act—kind or otherwise—comes back to you manyfold. The kinder you are to others, the more love and kindness will return to you. Conversely, no matter how justified an unkind word or action may feel to you, it will return to you with a vengeance a thousandfold.

This law is in place to introduce us to ourselves. No matter how we try to escape ourselves, we can't. Whatever we do, whatever action we take, whatever energy we express to one another in the world, eventually we'll experience the same energy returning to us from those around us. We get what we give, so it only takes giving fully of our heart and Spirit to others to ensure our complete happiness and joy.

My spiritual teacher, Dr. Tully, once told me that one of the best ways to be kind is not to stir up the emotional waters of others. When we rouse someone else's emotions, we cause stress, anxiety, defensiveness, worry, and fear to erupt from the person's ego. These are some of the most painful vibrations to course through our human nervous system. To set these turbulent waters into motion in others is hurtful, yet we do this all the time. And we do it in such subtle ways that we aren't even aware we're doing it.

We stir up stress and fear in others when we raise our voice or speak too harshly. We stir the waters of others' emotions when we snap at them; speak impatiently; and communicate with a prideful, irritated, or condescending tone. We may not even be aware that our tone is harsh, yet we still unleash a tsunami of fear and anxiety in others through a careless word or sarcastic remark.

For example, I was waiting to board an airplane in Chicago several years ago when it was announced that the plane was unexpectedly delayed. The gate area was full, and clearly the news upset everyone waiting to get on the flight.

One of the passengers was a young mother traveling with her three- or four-year-old son. I could tell by his energy and behavior that this was his first flight and he was extremely excited about his upcoming adventure. While we sat waiting to board the plane, he talked enthusiastically to his mom about where he would sit and how he would look out the window once in the air. He wondered if he would be able to see the ground after takeoff and if everyone was going to the same place. He freely shared his anticipatory musings as he prepared himself for this big adventure. It was evident that his heart was wide open with delight.

His mother listened and smiled halfheartedly, as this conversation had clearly been going on for some time, maybe even days. But when she heard that the flight was delayed, she became rather irritated that her plans had been interrupted. Meanwhile, her son, who didn't understand that there had been a change in plans, kept on talking excitedly about his adventure. He did, that is, until she snapped: "Be quiet, please—I'm listening to the agent."

From the look on his face, she might as well have thrown ice water on it. He was so shocked and hurt by her tone of voice that he blinked and became perfectly still for a moment. Then suddenly his eyes welled up with tears, and he looked away quickly, perhaps for somewhere to hide.

Her thoughtless remark felt so harsh to him that it cut right through to his heart and wounded him. It left him confused and devastated, and it broke my heart to watch. The worst of it was that his mother was so intent on listening to the announcements that she didn't even notice how hurt her son had felt over her impatient remark. She missed it altogether.

I'm not sharing this story to tell on a bad mother, but rather because the minute I saw it happen, I remembered a thousand occasions when I, too, had been guilty of the same with my own daughters when they were young. I, too, have let life overwhelm me or rob me of my peace at times and have lashed out unconsciously as a result of my own anxiety.

I felt sad for the boy, but for the mother as well. She would suffer for this, too, because she'd be deprived of his light. Right then I grabbed my cell phone and called both of my daughters, one after the other, to say how sorry I was for all the times I'd spoken to them harshly or unkindly in the past.

They both laughed at me and said, "Don't worry about it now—it's okay." But until I said I was sorry, I felt as though my past unkind behavior was robbing me of some of the closeness and light I want to share with my children today. I felt better undoing a little of my own unkindness in that moment. It calmed the emotional waters in me.

Being kind takes discipline and only flows with ease if you're committed to loving and living your Spirit over your ego. In fact, one way you can definitely tell whether you're disconnected from your Spirit is to notice if you're being unkind. The Spirit is sensitive and aware of the Divine in all, so it chooses only to be caring. To act in an unkind way isn't appealing to the Spirit; it only appeals to your false, impatient ego self.

To be genuinely kind to others, you must start being genuinely kind to yourself. If you're insensitive and impatient with yourself, your internal vibration will be stressed and resentful. If you're stressed and uncaring toward yourself, it can't help but ripple out toward other people. Kindness toward self is the gift that keeps on giving. To be kind to yourself is to value and love your Spirit and fuel your inner light.

Kindness is a choice to honor the Divine in all, including you. This takes practice until it becomes a habit. Summon the discipline within to develop the habit of kindness toward yourself and others. Stop allowing the ego to abuse you, and take the time to be kind every chance you get.

Being kind to yourself starts by checking in with your basic needs. Are you eating food that's good for you? Are you eating often enough? Too often? Are you going to bed early enough? Do you have a good pillow? Are you taking time to relax? These are simple kindnesses that ease the harshness of life and feed your Spirit.

Another very basic aspect of kindness to self is to afford ourselves healthy boundaries and be clear and direct in communicating them to others. Most of us were taught that we have no right to personal boundaries and that saying no or respecting our own needs is selfish. Fortunately, that school of self-sacrificing thought is starting to dissipate, and we're now being encouraged to be clear and ask for what we need without hesitation or guilt. Even so, old habits die hard. If all we've ever seen or been told is that to be loving, we must give of ourselves to the point of self-annihilation, then coming to comfortably know and exert our personal needs and boundaries may be overwhelming and take some encouragement.

A young client told me of her difficulty in college because all her dorm mates drank excessively, smoked pot, and were extremely noisy and aggressive night after night, often tumbling into her room with their parties. Not sharing in their excesses yet not wanting to be "unkind" to her college friends, she didn't speak up or even register her objections with her fellow students about their antics. The less she said, the worse it got.

When their drunken stupors passed, her college friends often told her how much they appreciated her and how great she was for putting up with their self-destructive behaviors and letting others intrude upon her space. Yet somehow this didn't feel as good to her as she thought it would or should. In fact, she felt worse.

Although she perceived her tolerance of others as kind, her insensitivity to herself was abusive. She lost sleep night after night and paid the price in class. Being unkind to herself built up a slow-burning rage in her, which she finally unleashed not only on her dorm mates, but also on her younger sister and parents.

Eventually they'd had enough. That's when they sent her to me. They were tired of her anger and didn't know where it came from or how to protect themselves from it. She didn't either, so she asked me. I helped her recognize how unconscious and insensitive she was being to her Spirit by not communicating her limits to those she had to live with at school. Not only was it unkind to her, it made her unkind toward her family, and ultimately even strangers. It even hurt her dorm mates, because it's not kind to give others permission to walk all over you and encourage their egos to run amok with indifference and insensitivity to the people around them. Her so-called kindness encouraged her dorm mates' rude and imposing behaviors and encouraged them to be abusive. All of this could be kindly stopped with simple clarity. In her case, a mere "Hey guys, take it outside—I'm sleeping" might be all it would take to turn the situation around.

This is where I suggested that she recognize just how kind it is to have boundaries and say no quickly to some things in life. She listened and tried it. It was uncomfortable to speak up, but the first time was the last. Her friends got the message and took the party elsewhere. She felt better, and so did they.

If we don't afford ourselves healthy boundaries with others, we get overwhelmed and our feelings become toxic. This often leads us to inappropriately lash out at the wrong people, setting up a vicious cycle.

To say no isn't unkind. But to say yes when you mean no *is* unkind because it's misleading and confusing to others. You may say yes to the uncomfortable or compromising situation in the moment, but you'll definitely want some payback for that later, often when others least expect it or aren't prepared to give anything. To say no without drama or hesitation is a great blessing to all. When you live with healthy boundaries, you create the opportunity to connect with people honestly, without confusion or manipulation. Everyone feels safer and more grounded.

The importance of healthy boundaries can't be overstated. It's up to you to be clear about what feels right and true for you. Only then can you communicate your boundaries to others, rather than hoping that they figure them out for you. They won't, and it's unkind to ask them to try. It's far more loving to be clear and direct than it is to beat around the bush being vague or passive-aggressive in an attempt to manipulate others into meeting your needs.

Getting in touch with your boundaries is actually simpler than it sounds. Usually, a boundary has been crossed or ignored if you find yourself feeling irritated, angry, or frustrated. When these feelings arise, simply check in with yourself and ask a few questions:

- Have I said yes when I mean no?

- Have I failed to express my need?

- Have I gone along with something that doesn't honor my Spirit?

- Have I stayed in a situation when my Spirit wanted to leave?

- Am I willing to change that now?

- Have I made a decision that will take the pressure off?

These simple questions begin to work your awareness muscles and help you better tune in to what's kind and loving to your Spirit.

The moment you do what feels kind to your Spirit, the Universe will help you build healthier boundaries. Until you decide that it's okay to communicate your limits, nothing can change at all.

Another way to be fundamentally kind to yourself is to make choices that take the pressure off of your life rather than living in a state of constant emergency and drama as you move from day to day. Kindness is rooted in being practical. The more grounded and realistic you are in your commitments, the less stressed-out you are— hence, the more peaceful and kind you can be.

A favorite story of mine involves a time when His Holiness the Dalai Lama was interviewed on television. The interviewer asked him what he does to stay so centered and friendly and loving all the time. He simply answered, "I leave for appointments early."

Expecting a profound metaphysical answer, the interviewer was shocked to hear something so basic to staying calm. Yet it's the small daily decisions we make that compose the tenor and tone of our lives. If we leave early for appointments, we stay calm and centered in Spirit. If we leave late, we set ourselves up for drama, fear, and stress of the ego.

The kindness the Dalai Lama chose for himself by leaving early is simple. By pacing himself and managing his affairs in a realistic timetable, he took an important step in being able to be kind to all. When we pace ourselves properly so that there's no rush, we relax. We leave stress and enter the Spirit of grace.

Overall, kindness is an awareness that we're all sensitive Divine Beings caught in a learning aiming toward our mastery. It's love in action. It's the accelerant for our souls' desire to grow and expand our peace.

To be kind is to slow down, relax, and let quality more than quantity be our highest goal in life. Know that simple kindness begets kindness. It ripples into the world like waves in the ocean. Your kindness sets off that in another, which then does the same in another, and together we gracefully elevate the tone of the world to be respectful and loving to all.

Kindness is less a doing and more of an allowing. It *allows* mistakes. It *allows* time and patience. It *allows* encouragement and forgiveness. It *allows* for us all to pursue our learning curve without shame or fear. It *allows* the dignity of Spirit to lead life.

Allow yourself more kindness. Afford more of it to others. It's the one self-loving expression of Spirit that keeps on giving.

Simple Practice: Follow Your Intuition

The final and perhaps most empowering of all decisions you can make when it comes to loving yourself and living your Spirit is to follow your intuition and allow it to guide your life.

Every one of us has been endowed with a sixth sense that originates in the center of our heart. This sense is our *intuition,* which literally means "inner teacher." This inner teacher is the voice of our most authentic self, our Spirit. It's Source wisdom guiding our lives. To follow our intuition is to claim our Divine nature and live it. It comes as a gut feeling, an "Aha," a sense, a hit, or a flash. For some it's subtle; for others, it's a bit stronger . . . yet, no matter how it feels, it's there for us all.

The first step in trusting your vibes is to recognize that your intuition is your greatest asset and give it the respect it deserves. Once you honor your vibes, trusting them becomes easier. Your intuition speaks from your heart and your Spirit. The simplest way to access your intuition is to ask your heart for guidance, then listen.

You can easily get an answer from your heart by placing your hand directly over it, saying out loud "My heart says _____," and then filling in the blank.

It helps, of course, if you feel safe and nonthreatened as you ask, so give yourself the support and privacy you need to do this without distraction. Make sure that the kids are occupied, turn off your cell and home phones, and shut off the TV. This technique works best when you respond out loud. When the heart speaks, you feel the energy and vibration of your Spirit. It's very different from your ego mind—it's calm, clear, and peaceful because it's connected to Divine mind.

Here are some other ways to tune in to yourself:

— **Take time.** Another technique for accessing your intuition is to give yourself a little time before responding to a situation. Use this period to go for a short walk, write for a few minutes in a journal, meditate, or simply have a cup of tea and get in touch with how you feel. The ego is an intense and often overzealous machine that distracts you from your intuitive feelings. It's important to be aware of these distractions and get around them by taking a few minutes to turn inward and listen.

— **Breathe.** A few rounds of deep breathing also help you tune in to your intuition. It takes only a few moments to inhale through your nose, then release the sound "Ah" out through the mouth. This technique quiets the ego and gives an opening to the heart.

— **Check in.** Another tip for accessing intuition is to avoid asking others for their opinions before you check in with your intuition first. Even the most well-intentioned input can distract you from tuning inward.

— **Talk it over.** Verbalizing your feelings helps a lot when attempting to hone your sixth sense. Sometimes you can actually tell if a particular decision or path is right or not by simply listening to the vibration as you speak it.

Recently I hired a young college student (who came highly recommended) to do some video work for me. As I was telling my manager about him, every cell in my body felt that this kid wasn't going to do a good job. I tried to ignore this, but the more I talked about him, the more strongly I felt that he was going to be a disappointment.

Trusting my hesitation, I changed my expectations about him on the spot. I went ahead with the video shoot, but I didn't press for a second one. Instead, I asked to view the first. Sure enough, what he had done was a bust. But because I'd trusted my intuition, I wasn't surprised, so I wasn't upset. Wasting no more time, I quickly changed course and hired someone far more capable for the job the next day. Had I not discussed it, I might not have tuned in as quickly to the message that the young man was wrong, wasting a lot more time. Having talked it over, I was guided by my intuition and it was no big deal.

—**Journal.** Writing in a journal hones your intuition quite nicely as well. Simply jot down the statement: "My intuition tells me _____," and then write in a stream-of-consciousness fashion for 10 to 15 minutes. You'll be delighted by what your intuition reveals.

A client from England who was a doctor tried this technique. She wrote:

> *My intuition tells me to stop my private practice and move to New Zealand. My intuition tells me I am unhappy in traditional medicine and want to work with holistic healing practices instead. My intuition tells me my parents and peers will be appalled at my ideas. My intuition tells me to do it anyway. My intuition tells me I will be very happy and successful if I do.*

Surprised by this exercise, she suddenly realized just how unhappy in her work she was. Her writing told her that she had options and secret dreams and that they lay just below the surface of her mind. It also revealed just how much she lived for the approval of others and ignored her own happiness.

This realization shook her up. She took it to heart and quit her job. As forewarned, her parents and friends thought she'd lost her mind and highly disapproved. Yet, assured by her intuition, she got past their objections and did move to New Zealand. She found easier, lighter work as a massage therapist. She also found herself a wonderful husband and became the mother of two sons. She said that she never regretted her decision to change direction, and she never looked back. To this day, she journals for guidance and finds that it's always there.

When *you* journal for guidance, don't analyze your responses. Simply write down your feelings and do nothing, at least not at first, unless your intuition is screaming to change course—as it was for my client in England—and unless time is of the essence . . . then act.

For example, a client wrote: "My intuition tells me to go see my mother before it's too late." Her mom had been quite sick for a while, and she knew that she would eventually succumb to her illness, yet my client wasn't aware that death would come so soon. She took the advice and left the next weekend to see her mom. Two days after she returned from the trip, her mother died of a massive heart attack, something completely different from her ongoing illness.

The key to honing intuition is first to simply express your inner feelings and then to observe how they energetically feel to you. Your body responds immediately to your sixth sense. True intuition, once acknowledged, usually leaves you with a sense of calm or satisfaction, even when it calls for a change of plans. You feel peaceful in your bones once you allow your Spirit to speak and be heard.

Tuning in to your intuition is only half the equation when it comes to self-love and being true to your Spirit, however. The greater challenge is to act on your vibes when they do arise. So many people do want to trust their intuition but never get around to it, only to regret it later. Don't be one of these people!

Start by acting on your intuition in little nonthreatening ways every day. For example, if your intuition says to take a different way home from work one day, then do. Don't waste time wondering why. When it comes to something small and seemingly inconsequential, give your vibes a chance to influence you. Only then will you learn to trust them. Besides, to follow your vibes in little ways keeps life fun, fresh, spontaneous, and exciting. It gives your ego a break and your Spirit a chance to lead.

The operative word here is *trust*. By heeding your intuition in little ways, you begin to gain the confidence to trust it in more pressing life matters.

Getting in better touch with your intuition and following it in nonthreatening ways trains your ego to step back and invites your Spirit to take the reins. In this way the two aspects of self—ego mind and Divine mind—learn to cooperate with each other and become friends. The ego is calmed by the positive benefits that following intuition brings. And your Spirit is at ease as it assumes its proper role as the guiding light of your life.

This is the simplest way of all to live, with head and heart in alignment. Following your intuition won't necessarily eliminate all of your woes, but it will ease a lot of them. And it will also better allow you to navigate through life's more difficult passages.

Your intuition is the guiding voice of your life. It's the light in the dark and the best authority in all matters. Trusting and acting on it affirms that you are a Divine Being, guided by Source, and not a victim of random chaos in a crazy world. You leave the world of fear—or at least it greatly recedes. With your increased peace and clarity, you begin to understand that the answer is simple: The way to love yourself is to live your Spirit. And the way to live your Spirit is to always and in all ways trust your vibes.

Epilogue

Last week as I was bringing this book to its conclusion, I asked my Spirit what she thought was the simplest way to love yourself and live *your* Spirit. I listened for a moment, and this is what I heard:

Sonia, life's a theater. As souls, we come here to learn to live, love, create, and forgive. Each lifetime is like a play. We each take on various roles in it: Some are heroes; others, heroines . . . some, villains and victims; others, clowns and fools. It doesn't matter which role we play, because by the end, we've played them all. The only thing that really matters after all is said and done is that we remember that it's all a Divine play and we, as Spirit, are the creative writers, directors, and actors in every scene.

The point of the play is to remember that we are here to create as Divine Beings—and to forgive all the bad plays we've ever written and starred in, and try again. There will always be another scene, another chance, another opportunity to get it right, because we have free will and can do it all over another way if we choose. And the right play, the best play, is the one in which we love with abandon, laugh at everything, forget and forgive quickly and completely, and are eternally grateful for the chance we've been given to play in this Divine theater called life in the first place.

For all I've said in this book, I think that my Spirit— the Spirit we all share—summarizes it best and makes it very simple. . . . Don't you?

Acknowledgments

I would like to dedicate this book to my family, both bloodline and soul family.

This includes my husband, Patrick; and two daughters, Sonia and Sabrina, who understand and support my mission and share me with so many without complaint.

To my mother and father, Sonia and Paul Choquette, who taught me early in life that joy is our Divine right and something to claim for myself.

To my sisters and brothers, Cuky, Stefan, Neil, Anthony, Noelle, and Soraya, who know and reflect my Spirit and make me laugh like no others.

To my Translucent You family, Cuky, Mark, Karl, Kyle, Crystal, Michelle, Debra, Kimo, and Bradd, who challenge me always to be my best, and fearlessly celebrate life with me.

To my artistic support, Julia Cameron and Linda Kahn, who help shape my literary ideas into real books.

To my Hay House family, Reid, Louise, Mollie, Jill, Alex, Nancy, Chris, Adrian, Margarete, the publicity team, and all the behind-the-scenes people, for believing in me in every way, treating me like royalty, and honoring my Spirit.

To my friends and neighbors, here and in France, who create community and celebration with me year-round. To LuAnn Glatzmaier, for cheering me on when I thought the answer wasn't so simple, and reminding me it is. To Erica Trojan and Jessica Burnett, for guiding me as I sounded out my ideas on this book. To Valentina Grodzena, for keeping my home grounded and sound. To Ann Kaiser, for swiftly and lovingly translating my jumbled notes into a working manuscript. And a special and heartfelt thanks and acknowledgment to Ryan Kaiser, my manager and business partner, who makes everything in my working life extremely simple. You are the greatest.

About the Author

Sonia Choquette is a world-renowned author, storyteller, vibrational healer, and six-sensory spiritual teacher in international demand for her guidance, wisdom, and capacity to heal the soul. She's the author of several best-selling books, including *Diary of a Psychic, Ask Your Guides,* and *Trust Your Vibes;* and numerous audio programs and card decks. Sonia was educated at the University of Denver and the Sorbonne in Paris, and holds a Ph.D. in metaphysics from the American Institute of Holistic Theology. She resides with her family in Chicago.

Websites: **www.soniachoquette.com** and **www.trust yourvibes.com**

Notes

Notes

Notes

Notes

Notes

Notes

Notes

Notes

Notes

Notes

Hay House Titles of Related Interest

YOU CAN HEAL YOUR LIFE, the movie,
starring Louise L. Hay & Friends
(available as a 1-DVD program and an expanded 2-DVD set)
Watch the trailer at: **www.LouiseHayMovie.com**

❀

GRATITUDE: A Way of Life, by Louise L. Hay and Friends

*HAPPINESS NOW!: Timeless Wisdom for Feeling
Good FAST,* by Robert Holden, Ph.D.

LOVE HAS FORGOTTEN NO ONE: The Answer to Life,
by Gary R. Renard

*MESSAGES FROM SPIRIT: The Extraordinary Power
of Oracles, Omens, and Signs,* by Colette Baron-Reid

*MYSTICAL TRAVELER: How to Advance to a
Higher Level of Spirituality,* by Sylvia Browne

*POWER OF THE SOUL: Inside Wisdom for
an Outside World,* by John Holland

*RELAX—You May Only Have a Few Minutes Left:
Using the Power of Humor to Overcome Stress
in Your Life and Work,* by Loretta LaRoche

REPETITION: Past Lives, Life, and Rebirth,
by Doris Eliana Cohen, Ph.D. (available November 2008)

*TRANSFORMING FATE INTO DESTINY:
A New Dialogue with Your Soul,* by Robert Ohotto

*THE WISDOM OF YOUR FACE: Change Your
Life with Chinese Face Reading!* by Jean Haner

All of the above are available at your local bookstore,
or may be ordered by contacting Hay House (see last page).

❀